DREAMBODY

The Vital Centers in the Human Body

Arnold Mindell

DREAMBODY
The Body's Role in Revealing the Self

Edited by
Sisa Sternback-Scott and Becky Goodman
Introduction by Marie-Louise von Franz

SIGO PRESS

© Copyright 1982 by Arnold Mindell

Sigo Press
77 North Washington Street, 201, Boston, Massachusetts 02114

Publisher and General Editor: Sisa Sternback-Scott
Associate Editors: Lindsay Smith
                  Becky Goodman

Library of Congress Cataloging in Publication Data

Mindell, Arnold, 1940–
   Dreambody, the body's role in revealing the self.

   Bibliography: p. 201.
   Includes index.
   1. Mind and body.   2. Self.   3. Health.   4. Jung,
C.G. (Carl Gustav) 1875–1961.   I. Sternback-Scott, Sisa.
II. Goodman, Becky.   III. Title.
BF161.M56 1982   150.19'54   82-3239
ISBN 0-938434-05-5   AACR2
ISBN 0-938434-06-3 (pbk.)

Cover illustration by Linda Weidlinger
Cover design by John Coy
Frontispiece: From the William Law Edition of Jacob Boehme

Set in Garamond ITC typeface.
Printed in the United States of America by Peace Press.

CONTENTS

ILLUSTRATIONS*

*Illustration credits appear on page 208.

ACKNOWLEDGMENTS

I am very indebted to Marie-Louise von Franz and to Nora Mindell for having discussed with me various parts of this work that are based on Jungian theory. Roy and Sherry Freeman were essential as listeners and debaters at crucial moments in the development of *Dreambody*. I am grateful to Carl Mindell for introducing me to meditation and to Barbara Croci for her help with yoga. Vernon Brooks was of great assistance in the original editing of this work, and Grace Darling Griffin supported me with encouragement when I could no longer go on. Without the insights and editorial assistance of Sisa Sternback-Scott and Becky Goodman, this work would never have come into being. The Research Society for Jungian Psychology, Zurich, supported my work financially during its experimental phase. Finally, thanks are due to Marijke and J. L. Boele van Hensbroek of Lemniscaat Publishers, Rotterdam, for recommending that *Dreambody* be used as the foundation for a less scholarly book that focuses mainly on case material.

INTRODUCTION

Arnold Mindell's book on the Dreambody appears at a time when it is much needed. A great deal of interest in body work has sprung up, especially in the United States. This in itself can be regarded as a psychological symptom: too many people soar high up above reality in intuitive flights, or they live completely in their heads. Scientific theories, ideological "-isms," foreign religious teachings and the like sweep them off the ground, and the process of increasing urbanization everywhere estranges most people from their mother, the Earth. No wonder that our bodies and our physical instincts react.

This book is, in a way, the story of how Dr. Mindell, an intuitive himself, has reconquered this ailing realm of our life. His idea of a "Dreambody," a re-formulation of the age-old idea of a "subtle body," seems to me to be of essential importance. There is in this concept a step forward into unknown territory: the relation of body and psyche.

The book indicates that dreams pattern body processes, but an immense task still lies ahead here: to explore the question of whether certain archetypal images refer to special organic realms, and the question of whether these relationships—if they exist—are synchronistic or regular. Dr. Mindell's idea of letting the symptoms of the body speak for themselves by way of self-amplification seems to me to be especially helpful as a tool for exploring these questions further in an empirical way. (We possess a great many religious systems that *teach* such relationships, but as Westerners we need more empirical, detailed confirmation in order to believe in them.)

Most of the modern body work known to me is basically materialistic in outlook; even many of the Eastern teachings have taken that turn too. A viewpoint that tries to keep a balance between mind and body is very much needed. Every dream image can thus be seen as belonging to that in-between realm, referring equally to the mind and to the physiological body. I therefore hope that Dr. Mindell's pioneering work will encourage more research in this still unknown realm of experience.

Marie-Louise von Franz
March 1982
Zurich, Switzerland

Chapter 1
THE DREAMBODY

The dreambody, an idea inspired by C.G. Jung, has been intuited for centuries in many ancient religious systems, and parts of the dreambody have been touched upon by modern Reichians, gestalt psychologists and body therapists. This chapter discusses aspects of the dreambody in these therapies and historical references in shamanism and meditation rituals. Chapters 2, 3 and 4 investigate symbols of the dreambody as they appear in fairy tales and myths. Chapters 5 and 6 deal with changes in modern psychological theory and practice that result from the dreambody discovery.

The dreambody has so radically changed my practice of psychology that today terms such as dream and body work, which had a very specific meaning for me at one time, seem embarrassing to use and no longer apply to what I do. I retain these terms, however, because they refer to known aspects of psychotherapy, to psychologies that focus in a more or less predetermined way upon dreams.

I first became interested in the psyche-matter interaction years ago when I began studying theoretical physics and practicing Jungian psychology. But it was not until I became mildly ill some ten years ago that I began to ground my speculations about mind-body coupling in practical terms. Fate showed me that to unravel the mystery of psycho-physical reality in a personal way, I had to begin with the body. I could scarcely have imagined at that time that a mode of body work and a theory of physiological processes would grow out of that experimental period. Little did I guess that the world of the body is as vast as the realm of dream symbols and even less explored in modern psychology!

As my interest in physiology grew, my frustration also multiplied. Why could I not deal with body problems with the same facility that characterized my dream work? I tended to intellectualize severe body problems instead of experiencing their potent reality.

I doubt that I would have surmounted the impasses or found the courage to enter into the dimly lit regions of somatic experience if I had not been working with terminally ill patients at that time. They initiated me into modes of nonverbal communication whose significance I otherwise would have overlooked. The lessons they taught me reopened my relationship to my self and other analysands. In particular, these patients showed me how to "amplify" somatic processes, and helped me to define the dreambody.

I suspect that C.G. Jung was hinting at dreambody work when he wrote in his autobiography that it is important for a therapist to put his or her own training aside and to develop psychology anew with each new patient. But it is difficult to realize Jung's recommendation in practice because of the unpredictability of individual situations encountered in analysis. Some people bring pressing love problems to therapy while others wish to concentrate on immense dreams, focus on body problems or discuss startling synchronicities. Obviously, working with dream symbols and body problems will be required by anyone interested in meeting Jung's challenge to continuously recreate psychology.

Each new moment is theoretically adventurous and experimentative. Sometimes work focuses on the "therapist," sometimes on the "patient." We can choose to work in or out of the office, talk or be silent, sit or walk, dance or work on dreams. We may make appointments or leave them up to the moment spontaneously.

However intuitive and grandiose an open attitude to analysis may appear, it is not simple to attain. Dealing fluidly with material which appears in the moment and not repressing specific events, requires self-knowledge, vast study and extensive training. I remember for example that before I felt at home in the world of dreams, I had to suffer through thousands of hours of dream analysis, labor over methods of imagination, association and amplification. Today amazing dreams still unsettle me! Tuning into body phenomena also requires a great deal of expertise.

Elements of the dreambody appear in body images, rituals and physical therapies practiced by yogis, shamans and medicine men. Shamanic healing in general employs altered states of consciousness, active imagination and biofeedback in order to cure illness in a given patient. Various imaginary causes are described in the literature as the origins of illness. They run the gamut from jealousy of a friend, the ill will of a sorcerer, and attacks by a spirit, to the ghostly visitations of a recently deceased person.

In this chapter, we look briefly at the best known Eastern body rituals and their derivatives—today's Western psychophysical therapies. The oldest body therapies still in use today are practiced in India, China and Tibet. Yoga was apparently originally shamanistic.[1] Consciousness for a yogi means dreambody awareness achieved by working through body knots and spasms with the help of hatha yoga.[2] The yogi knows the dreambody as his *purusha,* the meditation experience arising from breathing disciplines such as *pranayama.*

Ayurveda,[3] India's ancient medical procedure, employs yoga to combat pain; pain results from unconsciousness of the *purusha* or from worldly attachments. *Ayurveda* also employs causal procedures; it uses herbs and a social philosophy to treat diseases that stem from any number of problems such as ignorance or personal karma, tension caused by social demands, improper treatment of the real body, or even invasion by spirits like bacteria.[4]

Like Tantric yoga, Siddha yoga perceives body life as the action of a somatically experienced Shakti, namely the so-called Kundalini. Hence yogis attempt to contact, awaken, and com-

[1]Mircea Eliade, *Yoga: Immortality and Freedom.*
[2]A good beginning book on hatha yoga is Alain's *Yoga for Perfect Health.* Authentic material can be found in Patanjali's *Yoga-sutras.*
[3]C. Dwarakanath, *Introduction to Kayachikitsa.*
[4]Ibid.

bat this energy through meditation,[5] sexual stimulation, and physical exercise.[6] The awakened or enlightened individual has intimate contact with his freed dreambody energies.

An imbalance of body energies is believed to be a prime cause of disease in Indian and Chinese medical theory. The Chinese medical practitioner typically uses acupuncture to increase or decrease the yin or yang energy in the meridians carrying Tao through the body.[7] He uses meditation and diet[8] (depending on the yin or yang energy content of a given food) and also studies the seasons (and times) to determine what therapy would be most useful.[9] He knows the gods of the body who preside over the different organs as residing dignitaries.[10] The Chinese doctor must be in Tao himself as well. Therefore he makes a diagnosis (by means of differential pulse measurements)[11] only at special early hours in the morning when his own health is in perfect condition.

The Tibetan doctor takes synchronicity more fully into diagnostic account than his Indian and Chinese colleagues, and will even give his patient a poor prognosis if he himself is in a bad mood when the messenger arrives announcing the patient's illness. He may also make a diagnosis on his way to see the patient depending on various omens.[12] The patient's body or dreambody is everywhere for the Tibetan doctor.

Indian, Chinese, and Tibetan medicine all employ out-of-body states which occur, for example, after prolonged meditation. The religious experience accompanying these states is interwoven with medical techniques and body therapies to create a state of health which is identical to the immortal body. Healing is a secondary goal accompanying self-realization; the

[5]The best source I have found on Buddhist meditation for Western thought is Joseph Goldstein's *The Experience of Insight: A Natural Unfolding*. Undoubtedly the best in general is Shunryu Suzuki's *Zen Mind, Beginner's Mind*.
[6]See Arthur Avalon, *The Serpent Power*.
[7]A simple, direct do-it-yourself acupressure kit is J.V. Cerney's *Acupuncture Without Needles*.
[8]Only the original description of Chinese meditation does justice to this specialized art. See Lu K'uan Yü, *Taoist Yoga: Alchemy and Immortality*.
[9]*The Yellow Emperor's Classic of Internal Medicine*.
[10]See Rolf Homann, *Die wichtigsten Körpergottheiten im Huan't'ing Ching*.
[11]See, for example, *The Yellow Emperor's Classic of Internal Medicine*. We must ask what the doctor is measuring—certainly not the detailed structure of the patient's heart; rather the overall depressiveness, overexcitement or harmony of the nervous system is discovered.
[12]Rinpoche Rechung, *Tibetan Medicine*.

methods of achieving freedom from disease aim to transcend the body and time itself. Eastern ritual would call the dreambody the basic stuff of the body, the working substance that transforms into the experience of immortality. The dreambody thus goes by many names such as *Shakti* (the feminine goddess), *Kundalini* (or serpent power), *Mercury* (an imagined substance of Chinese alchemy), and *Chi* (a subtle energy). More essentially, however, the dreambody is inner body sensations and connected fantasies.

Hippocrates, the father of modern medicine, also believed in body energies—the *enormon* and the *physis*. These were powers responsible for the body's brute natural strength and its ability to heal itself. In the course of medical evolution, leading figures ignored Hippocrates' energy concepts, focusing instead on his "scientific" attitudes and his astute observation of diseases. In modern times, Wilhelm Reich, originally Freud's pupil, rediscovered this idea of subtle body energy.[13] Reich advanced psychoanalysis, venturing into somatic realms of pain and pleasure to which Freud had merely alluded.

Reich's concept of bio-energy is connected with his attempt to mobilize the blocked sexuality, anxiety, and aggressiveness stored in cramped muscular tensions which he termed "character armour." The neo-Reichians such as Alexander Lowen,[14] Stanley Keleman,[15] and John Pierrakos[16] developed therapies that differ from Reich's insofar as energy mobilization and analysis of character are more completely integrated and somewhat less reductive. The main goal of most neo-Reichians or bio-energetic therapists remains, however, to break down psychic and physical resistances, create a soft libidinous body and mind, and reduce problems to early childhood experience.

Lesser known modern body therapies such as the Alexander principle,[17] the Feldenkrais method[18] and Rolf's "structural integration"[19] are based on awareness and adjustment to the gravity field and inner tensions of the body. Although biofeed-

[13]Wilhelm Reich, *Character Analysis.*
[14]Alexander Lowen, *The Betrayal of the Body.*
[15]Stanley Keleman, *Your Body Speaks Its Mind.*
[16]John Pierrakos, *The Energy Field in Man and Nature.*
[17]Wilfred Barlow, *The Alexander Principle.*
[18]Moshe Feldenkrais, *Body and Mature Behavior.*
[19]Ida Rolf, "Structural Integration." See also Robert Prichard's article "Structural Integration (Rolfing)."

back,[20] which typically employs special instruments for amplifying body signals, has many similarities to Eastern meditation
systems, its aim is to control somatic signals, not to decode
their messages.

Fritz Perls, founder of modern gestalt therapy, would
definitely have been greeted as a colleague by a shaman in a
"primitive" culture.[21] Perls used identification and the dis-
identification of dream figures and body experiences to create
self-awareness. He borrowed from Moreno's "psycho-drama,"[22]
a method in which the dreamer uses himself and others to enact
dream contents.

Don Juan Matus, the American Indian shaman figure[23] in
Carlos Castaneda's saga, teaches body concepts such as doing,
not doing, personal power, dreaming up and the double, which
are dreambody phenomena. The American Indian's body concepts come from nomadic experiences with the environment;
the yogi's, from meditation.

In their exploration of psychosomatic medicine modern
Freudians have contributed greatly to making medicine aware
of the spirit in the body.[24] Neo-Freudians such as Franz Alexander have studied how behavior patterns may be associated with
medically defined diseases such as duodenal ulcers, hypertension, skin irritations and migraine headaches.

At the very beginning of his career, Jung investigated the relationship between psychology and physiology. He used a galvanometer to measure body responses during association tests,[25]
showing that the electrical behavior of the skin changed whenever complexes were present. Biofeedback researchers today
credit him with the discovery of what they call "skin talk."[26]
Although Jung's work is not noted for physical research, he
hypothesized that there was a chemical toxin behind schizo-

[20]*Biofeedback and Self-Control.*
[21]Frederick Perls, *Gestalt Therapy Verbatim.*
[22]J. L. Moreno, *Who Should Survive?*
[23]Carlos Castaneda, *The Teachings of don Juan; A Separate Reality; Journey
to Ixtlan; Tales of Power; The Second Ring of Power.*
[24]Franz Alexander, *Psychosomatic Medicine.*
[25]Charles Ricksher and C. G. Jung, "Further Investigations on the Galvanic
Phenomenon and Respiration in Normal and Insane Individuals," in C. G.
Jung, *Collected Works* (hereafter referred to as *CW*), Vol. 2.
[26]Barbara Brown, *New Mind, New Body,* pp. 69–70, 75–76.

phrenia, theorized about the mind-body relationship,[27] inter-preted dreams physiologically,[28] and studied the significance of Kundalini yoga.[29]

Perhaps Jung's most significant mind-body concept was his idea of synchronicity—that is, the meaningful relationship be-tween two or more events which have no apparent causal con-nection.[30] Though Jung used synchronicity and the concept of the psychoid unconscious[31] mainly in conjunction with para-psychological phenomena, modern Jungians such as Ziegler, Bach, Meier, Scott and Redfearn, and Lockhart have applied the concept of synchronicity to the relationship between spontane-ously appearing symbols and organic disorders.[32]

One of Jung's most practical concepts was his rediscovery and application of a prospective or finalistic point of view to psychology. He stepped out of his own medical heritage by showing that the psyche was not necessarily a pathological phenomenon but a meaningful realm of events with its own inner structure and flowing processes. He relativized healing concepts bent on changing life by discovering that the most frightening and compulsive psychic symptoms often contain specific goals and purposes.

In a similar manner, it has become clear to me that if we can temporarily restrain our conscious prejudices and view the body as a natural fact, we may thus free the body to express itself and demonstrate levels of meaning in its seemingly chaotic and destructive manifestations. Today we are knowledgeable about many curative techniques, but are urgently in need of more information about the potentially meaningful behavior of body states assumed to be pathological.

As this brief review indicates, both East and West have devel-oped causal and final approaches to the body in the course of

[27]C. G. Jung, *Letters,* Vol. 2, p. 44, in a letter to Raymond Smythies, February 1952.
[28]C. G. Jung, *CW,* Vol. 16, pars. 344f., and Vol. 18, fn. 15 and p. 102.
[29]"The Psychology of Eastern Meditation," *CW,* Vol. 11.
[30]"Synchronicity: An Acausal Connecting Principle," *CW,* Vol. 8.
[31]"Review of the Complex Theory," *CW,* Vol. 8.
[32]A. Ziegler, "A Cardiac Infarction and a Dream as Synchronous Events"; S. Bach, "Spontaneous Painting of Seriously Ill Patients"; C. A. Meier, "A Jungian Approach to Psychosomatic Medicine"; R. D. Scott, "Notes on the Body Image and Schema"; J. W. Redfearn, "The Patient's Experience of His Mind"; and Russell A. Lockhart, "Cancer in Myth and Dream."

their history. The study of body phenomena as they occur in practice brings together experimental techniques of the East with analytical approaches of the West.

When the dreambody manifests itself as an energetic charge shooting through the spine, we could call it by its ancient name, the Kundalini. When it is experienced as the essence of life, it is Mercury. When one visualizes its energy as streaming through the body, it is the twelve meridian system. If one sees it and acts on this vision we have gestalt identification. If one feels it as a cramp in breathing, it is called character armour. If one senses it and changes, we might speak of biofeedback. If it appears as a force pushing one in the stomach to do a new task, it is personal power. Obviously, we need a unified approach to the body.

Psychologists with sufficient training and flexibility to follow individual dreambody processes will discover that terms such as analysis, psychotherapy and body work must expand to the point where psychology allows the human being to touch upon every known theory and practice. Dreambody process may begin to "talk" in the style of gestalt, psychodrama, or active imagination or it may ask to be "Rolfed" with a penetrating massage. At other times or in other cases, the body may begin to spontaneously enact unknown postures such as Hatha yoga's asanas or enter into deep states of meditation characteristic of Zen. Balancing movements of the head characteristic of the Alexander technique also occur. Sometimes the body asks for a shaking typical of bioenergetic exercises; other times its spirit slips into a shamanistic dance. This spectrum of behavior is important for anyone interested in physiology. The Western therapist, in the face of the body work spectrum, needs to understand and accept forms of psyche and physical behavior that would be completely normal for a yogi, shaman or acupuncture specialist.

Understanding and accepting the dreambody as process, however, requires factual knowledge about its behavior and the courage to go to one's own limits in order to let the dreambody come into awareness. For the dreambody itself hovers between body sensation and mythical visualization.

Chapter 2
REAL BODY—DREAMBODY

THE BODY IN WESTERN RELIGION
Whereas the human body plays an important role in Buddhism, Hinduism, and Jainism as a tool to attain salvation, in Judaism and Christianity it plays an indirect, almost insignificant part in individuation. In the East the goal is to transform the body in order to transcend its limitations and to achieve liberation. But according to Judaism and Christianity, the theoretical body-mind unity man is born with is separated at death and comes together again only in the afterlife, at the end of time. The Western religious image of the body which is rejoined to the spirit in death is called the "glorified" or "resurrected body."[1] Jesus, standing as a light-body amidst auras and halos, is the outstanding image of the dreambody in Christianity.

The Old Testament view of the living body echoed in Christianity pictures the body as animated and vivified by the spirit. The body appears in Western religious theory as a sort of troublesome appendage quickly fitted into a doctrine in the form of a mysterious "glorified body" that can only be united with the spirit unconsciously—that is, in another world over which we have negligible control. Our Western religious doctrines coincide with the repressing of body signals in favor of visualizations dominated by mystical ideas such as ghosts, doubles, astral travel and out-of-body states. Thus far, to most Western people the dreambody is a mystical experience which does not occur in the here and now.

[1] *The Concise Encyclopedia of Living Faiths.* See Zachner's "Introduction" and R.J. Werblowsky's "Judaism, or the Religion of Israel," p. 34.

THE BODY IN WESTERN MEDICINE

Theological speculation about mind-body unity is reflected in Western thinking which has separated the body from the soul since the time of Descartes. This separation has made it possible to investigate the body as a machine, producing discoveries about a material world from which the spirit has been separated. The discovery of the microscope enabled scientists to locate pathological states and diseases at a cellular level, supporting the theory that the body was a machine run by electrical chemistry. Today medicine still conceives of the body as a rational organism whose behavior can be determined by the individual nature of its specific mechanical parts.

The gestalt psychologists of the late nineteenth century and the modern Freudian-oriented psychiatrists practicing psychosomatic medicine today have done much to reverse the idea that the body is the sum of its parts.[2] The gestalt psychologists view the body as a whole whose nature is more than the sum of its parts; in fact, the parts are governed by the totality. Freudians in particular have considered nonmaterial factors such as faith, stress and ego-rigidity in disease states. Yet psychosomatic medicine, still basically symptom-oriented, studies the body-spirit as if it were a controllable factor in the progression of specific diseases. The dreambody is not seen as an entity unto itself, with its own characteristics, but as a symptom to be overcome.

THE BODY IN PHYSICS

Like medicine, modern physics has been dominated by Greek and Christian thinking until modern times. Einstein himself said that Aristotle's conception of matter as a mechanical object moving in a geometrical space inhibited the development of physics for two thousand years. However, twentieth century research has forced physics to reject the Greek conception of geometrical space and matter.

Surprisingly enough, the new concepts of modern quantum mechanics are similar to Eastern views of matter.[3] Today physicists see matter as fields, energies and intensities, not as isolated, definite objects in space. Physics, the most rational branch of

[2]Franz Alexander, *Psychosomatic Medicine*, Chapter 1.
[3]Fritjof Capra, *The Tao of Physics*.

modern science, has produced a sort of subtle body view of nature. Matter is both solid and formless energy.

The appearance of the body, like all matter, depends on how we look at it. If we measure temperature by putting a thermometer under the arm, then the body appears in terms of temperature. If we close our eyes and attend to inner signals, then the body appears in terms of fantasies and sensations. I would define the real body as the result of objective physiological measurements, and the dreambody as the individual experience of the body.

The real body is the product of cultural concepts. Today, in the "civilized" world, the body is composed of heart, lungs, RNA, bacteria, cells and diseases. In contrast, the dreambody is created by individual experience, personal descriptions of signals, sensations and fantasies which do not necessarily conform to collective materialistic definitions. Both real body and dreambody descriptions are valid within their own observational realm. Confusion arises only when one body's description is treated more importantly than the other's or when questions pertaining to one body are asked about the other body.

The dependency of the body on the nature of observation recalls theoretical physics at the time when quantum physics was developed. In the beginning of the twentieth century, classical physics, which had ruled Western science for at least two hundred years, saw the world as a machine whose events could be predicted once their origins were given. Every event was ruled by some sort of mechanism which could be understood in terms of everyday experience. For example, molecules and atoms were imagined as baseballs which bounced off walls and obeyed the laws of cause and effect.

Exact measurements of elementary particles such as electrons demonstrated, however, that something was wrong with the mechanical conceptions of classical physics. The microscopic world of matter seemed to behave mercurially, as far as the observer in classical time and space was concerned. One could no longer prove that an electron went through one hole or another in a given experiment without severely disturbing the patterns created by the electrons streaming through the holes. Physicists such as Heisenberg, Bohr and Schrödinger daringly proposed certain formulas called "wave equations," which described the behavior of elementary particles. But other physicists who were emotionally bound to the classical world, where given causes created predictable effects, said that the wave equations could not be correct since they did not answer seemingly basic questions such as "Where does an electron go?"

After much deliberation Heisenberg finally answered these classical physicists by formulating his principle of uncertainty. He said that a question need not be answered if it cannot be experimentally tested. Classical physicists never considered their right to ask certain questions because they thought that the behavior of matter could not be disturbed by testing it. Heisenberg's principle implied, however, that it is impossible to create experiments that answer classical questions—such as finding out where an electron goes—without violently disturbing the free flow of the electrons. In one sense Heisenberg became matter's friend and protector, guarding its vulnerability against the insensitivity of classical physicists.

Quantum theory challenged classical physics, forcing it to realize that the observer plays a crucial role in the outcome of quantum events. Every observation disturbs events in at least two ways: by the choice of a particular apparatus to measure a special variable and by the use of energy for the observation itself. A third type of disturbance, the momentary psychic disposition of the observer at the time of the experiment (his dreams and body states), is not yet included in modern physics.

As far as *classical* physics is concerned, elementary quantum events look shy and other-worldly. They do not possess mechanical explanations and cannot be understood in terms of the causes and effects of everyday macroscopic experience. The behavior of elementary particles can only be formulated mathematically in terms of equations. The interpretation of these mathematics in terms of everyday life cannot be accomplished with accuracy. In other words, the language of quantum physics is symbolical; it is mathematical and has little relationship to ordinary experiences of the macroscopic world. For example, an electron is no longer pictured as a little round ball because no one knows exactly where the electron's boundaries are at any given time.

In the 1970s, physicists discovered that what they saw in their experiments strongly depended on what they decided to measure and on a given frame of consciousness. The so-called "bootstrap" physicists believe today that there are no fundamental laws of physics and that whatever they discover is a product of consciousness.[4] Quantum physics has made it necessary to consider ruptures and inconsistencies in Western ways of thinking and to reevaluate the origins of our thought. Physicists are just realizing that the very tendency to look for unified theories and search for perfect laws reflects the ancient Greek conception of the world. In old Greece the world consisted of geometrical symmetries, absolute laws and irreducible constituents of matter.[5] For Plato, God Himself was a geometer! It was not until Einstein that the relativity of geometrical concepts of the heavens was considered.

I discuss the struggles of quantum physics in validating itself because these struggles mirror the problems that arise when the dreambody is considered next to the concept of the "real body." Just as a material particle is no longer viewed as a little ball in space, so the idea of the real body can no longer be considered absolute. The very concept of a "real" body is classically Greek in origin. Spatial and temporal quantities such as body size and age are relative.

Questions about the origin of diseases are also classical and cannot be asked about the dreambody. Why? Because if these questions are asked, the dreambody experience is destroyed by forcing it to fit into collective definitions. The dreambody cannot be programmed like a computer to produce the answers that consciousness is interested in.

Questions about the health and illness of the body are not incorrect. They are simply classical, that is, possibly irrelevant to individual experience. Searching for the answers to classical medical questions—such as "Where did an illness come from?" —is oriented to ordinary consciousness and does not value dreams or body processes, which may not speak of illness at all. *Illness is an ego concept, a definition belonging to the realm of*

---

[4]Ibid. In my opinion, Capra has done an excellent job of presenting G.F. Chew's "bootstrap" concept which tests classical thinking.
[5]Ibid., pp. 168ff.

the real body. The existence of an illness may or may not be verified by dream material or individual body experience. If an "illness" produces symptoms strong enough to be experienced, *then* the dreambody has become active and is described in terms of these body experiences and dreams.

Whereas medicine might see different diseases existing in the body at one time in terms of different causes, in dreams and body work all physiological processes appear to be governed by single gestalts and their archetypal processes. These processes seem to choose any and all available signals or unstable organs for expression. This is why it is difficult or even fruitless to correlate individual organic problems generally with psychological behavior. If we want to get at the individual roots of body processes we must observe the personal, changing experience of the body.

To study the dreambody we have to let it manifest itself. Asking specific questions about its nature may even disturb it. Rational attitudes repress and frustrate dreambody processes just as a doubting, judgmental onlooker may inhibit a person's spontaneous behavior.

THE DREAMBODY AS VIBRATIONS AND FIELDS

Just as an elementary particle can be seen only indirectly by the streaking effects created by its movements in a cloud chamber, so the dreambody can be noticed but not understood in terms of the real body. The existence of the dreambody can be macroscopically tested and verified only by its effects on the "real" world. If we do not insist on an extraverted type of verification but ask about the nature of dreambody experience itself, then we may turn to literature about subtle body experiences. The yogi's subtle body is probably the best known experience of the dreambody (Fig. 1).

The gaseous, fluid and rhythmical nature of dreambody experienced by the yogi contrasts with the conscious concept of the body as an amazing machine with a hidden spirit. The flow and rhythm of the dreambody constitute a "field" experience, to use a term from physics. The field is a definite sensation of one's self as a process with only vague extremities in time and space. In contrast, the real body can be defined as an object with a certain weight, temperature, etc.

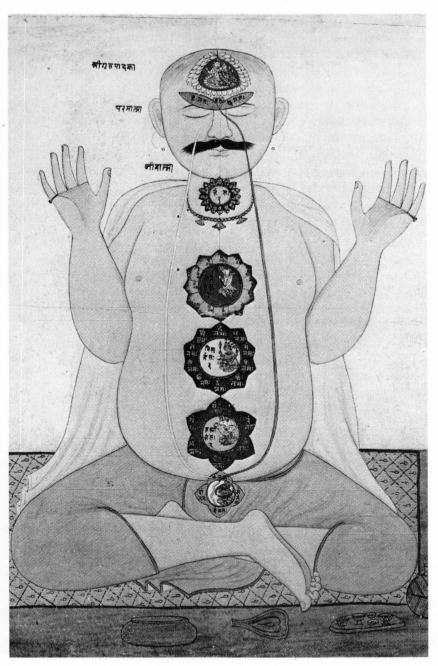

1. The Yogi's Subtle Body

The gaseous, vibratory, or field-like quality of the dreambody is analogous to the physicist's discovery that the elementary particles of matter are not material particles at all but aspects of the field's qualities. Instead of particles we have relatively high field densities at certain areas in space and time. These field densities and their associated discontinuities and intensities correspond to what classical physics calls matter. According to Albert Einstein, "We may regard matter as being constituted by the regions of space in which the field is extremely intense . . . There is no place in this new kind of physics both for the field and matter, for the field is the only reality."[6]

The idea of the dreambody as high intensity in space and time corresponds to one of Jung's intuitions about the nature of the soul. In his words,

> It might be that psyche should be understood as *unextended intensity* and not as a body moving with time. One might assume the psyche gradually rising from minute extensity to infinite intensity, transcending for instance the velocity of light and thus irrealizing the body.[7]

In another place he estimates the weight of the psyche as "very little" and speculates that it "belongs to micro-physics."[8]

The concept of the dreambody as a relatively high field intensity also corresponds to Taoist concepts. In Taoism the world is permeated by dragon lines of force (see Fig. 33, Chapter 3), which coalesce so to speak, in certain objects. The Tao is a force field permeating the universe. The human being in a certain place and time picks up a certain Tao and lives this in his own way.

The *I Ching* is also based on the idea of the Tao. Coins dropped at a given moment are oriented by the Tao of the place and time like a galvanometer which picks up the state of an electromagnetic field. I feel that the Tao is a pre-meaningful field, a sort of force either operating on the personality or radiated by it, a force which when made conscious reveals meaning. Unto itself, however, the Tao, or the field in which we live, is simply a presence characterizing a given moment in space and time.

[6]Ibid., p. 221.
[7]C.G. Jung, *Letters,* Vol. 2, p. 45, in a letter to John Smythies.
[8]C.G. Jung, *Letters,* Vol. 1, p. 394.

In Chinese philosophy, the field idea also appears in the concept of *Chi,* which means gas or ether and denotes the energy or breath that animates the universe.[9] The pathways of the Chi also go through the body. Acupuncture corrects any blocks in these channels so that the body may again flow with the Chi or Tao.

The flow in the Chi is basic to the Tai Chi, the Taoist dance of the warrior. Fritjof Capra, in his book *The Tao of Physics,* points out that the Chi (like the quantum field) is conceived as a "tenuous and nonperceptible form of matter which is present throughout space and can condense into solid material objects." Quoting Joseph Needham's description of the Chinese view of physical reality, Capra notes,

> The Chinese physical universe was perfectly continuous . . . Chi condensed in palpable matter was not particulate in any important sense, but individual objects acted and reacted with all other objects in the world . . . in a wave-like or vibratory manner dependent, in the last resort, on the rhythmic alternation at all levels of the two fundamental forces, the yin and the yang. Individual objects thus had their intrinsic rhythms. And these were integrated . . . into the general pattern of the harmony of the world.[10]

THE DREAMBODY AS DANCE

Understanding the dreambody requires a feeling for the field in which the body exists, or, formulated less classically, understanding the body requires experiencing the field of which the body is a part. A common way of experiencing this field is through creative dance, the motion of the body directed by the non-ego. Typically, creative dance is experienced as flow through the body; the earth vibrates, the air is electric, and a mysterious force seems to move one to life.

The rhythmical essence of the dreambody appears in the Tai Chi (Fig. 2), dervish ritual (Fig. 3), and the Indian philosophy of the Self, Shiva, the god of all. Shiva's dance (Fig. 4) is the dreambody's flow, the field's structure expressed in movement. According to an ancient Indian text,

> Nature is inert, and cannot dance till Shiva wills it. He rises from his rapture, and dancing sends through inert matter pulsing

9Capra, *The Tao of Physics,* p. 224.
10Ibid., p. 225.

2. Rhythm Essence of Tai Chi

waves of sound, and lo!, matter also dances, appearing as a glory
round about him. Dancing, he sustains its phenomena. In the
fullness of time, still dancing, he destroys all forms and names by
fire and gives new rest . . .[11]

In other words, when one becomes aware of the existence of
the dreambody, then it or Shiva eventually rises and the body
literally pulses with dance and sound. The spontaneity of dance
relativizes conscious life, i.e., forms and names. In this way the
body liberates itself from the mind's control and new rest is
achieved.

Dance is communion with the Self or "personal power," to
use a shamanistic term from Castaneda's don Juan. He speaks of
a "dance of power" in which the body reviews its entire history
and expresses its last message before death. Memories stored in

3. Dervish Ritual

the great muscles of the body arrange its motions while Death watches and waits until this last act, a dance, is accomplished.

The field of which the body is a part may be called the Tao, the power of the earth, the sun's radiation, or simply the changing seasons. Figure 5 shows dancers communing with and welcoming the seasons. When an evil spirit causes disease, the shaman dances to drive off the evil spirit (Fig. 6).

The person governed only by time and social pressure is not in contact with the body spirit or the Self and experiences him-

4. *Dancing Shiva*

5. *Dance to the Seasons*

6. *Shaman's Healing Dance*

self as a particle in a field, an object whose life is directed by outer circumstances and stressed by irreconcilable forces. In contrast, the individual who is aware of and manifests inner life dances and has a quantum experience of life.

For the psychologist, the physicists' description of the classical and quantum view of matter are projections of the ego's experiences of itself and the ego's experience of the Self. The unaware person experiences himself as a particle in the midst of an outer field and as a body plagued by disease. The more sensitive person experiences himself as the field itself and dances effortlessly.

For the dreambody, the material world and the real body appear as mental constructions responsible for inhibition and unhappiness. The real body seems to be created by the ego's fear, rigidity or stubbornness. From the viewpoint of ordinary consciousness, however, the dreambody appears to be a subtle body, a gaseous apparition deviating from and threatening reality.

THE DREAMBODY IN SHAMANISM

In the vocabulary of modern physics, or its amplification in terms of Eastern philosophy, the dreambody may be experienced as a relatively high intensity in a field with a given structure, flow and direction. If we study shamanistic experience of birth, death, drugs or illness we arrive at another description of the dreambody.

Don Juan describes the death experience and its transcendence in terms of dissociating and reassembling the personality with the help of what he calls the glue of life.[12] Dreambody consciousness is acquired through training the ego to be aware of the personality during dreaming, meditation, hypnogogic states and exhaustion, in which out-of-body experiences occur. Don Juan's training integrates death into life by making him conscious of his immortal Self, which don Juan calls the double.

According to don Juan, the purpose of life is to enable the "man of knowledge" to become conscious of his double, the personality which knows itself independently of the sleeping body during dreaming. The double is a term used by the ordinary man to describe the warrior's ability to leave his body and

[12]Carlos Castaneda, *Journey to Ixtlan.*

be in two places at one time or to travel backward in time. The warrior himself, however, barely knows about his double or its magical effects, since he concentrates only on one event at a time. The "fluid warrior" drops out of chronological time and focuses only on his own process, whatever that may be. An "impeccable warrior" knows about the double but does not "produce" it. It simply happens to him through being himself. The double is "nothing else than the warrior himself," the person who submits himself consciously to the flow of inner experience.

People who become "men of knowledge" have fibers radiating from their stomachs, making them look like "luminous eggs" to other men of knowledge who can "see." These field-like people differ in don Juan's perceptions from ordinary people or "phantoms" who possess no radiation and who are blind and eagerly attached to the world.

Psychologically speaking, the "man of knowledge" is an archetype of the individuated or self-actuated person, when these terms are understood in connection with a body that expresses itself, as well as a psyche that has become centered. The enlightened or completed person is one who lives the dreambody.

One finds the completed human being image in practically every shamanistic tradition. In yoga, for example, the man of knowledge appears as the yogi or guru, i.e., the one who has, according to the ancients, become a "dead man in life." In China, the realized individual is capable of allowing the spirit, or yang-light constellated by meditation, to radiate through the yin world, or unconsciousness and darkness. This yang energy is apparently the essence of the dreambody. According to the *Secret of the Golden Flower,* the yang energy wanders around the body, enters the liver at night and produces dreams. During the daytime this energy may appear as a third eye between the two real eyes of the meditator.[13] The initiate must learn to control the differentiating and discriminating power of yin consciousness so that the yang power may break through as the yellow flower. This breakthrough creates the dharma body which is later inhabited in death.

While the Chinese and Indian conceptions of the dreambody refer basically to states constellated by reduced consciousness,

[13]Mokusen Miyuki, "*The Secret of the Golden Flower,* Studies and Translation," p. 81.

don Juan's man of knowledge is a dreambody experience happening in sober wakefulness. Don Juan's nomadic Indian experience of the dreambody tends to be more extraverted than the yogi's introverted discovery of the dreambody occurring during meditation in an essentially more agrarian culture.

Nevertheless, all the yogic and shamanistic trainings encountered thus far seem to have one basic goal in common: the awareness of a dreambody which one may inhabit in an afterlife. In other words, dreambody awareness is a preparation for death and a living confrontation with the timeless nature of the personality.

THE DREAMBODY AS CLAIRVOYANT VISION

The idea of the dreambody as a field intensity, or double, can be found throughout the world. Western occultists call the dreambody the "etheric body" or the "fine-matter body."[14] In Egypt, the soul transcending the body in death is called the *Ka Soul,* the equivalent of *Doppelgänger* in old Europe. The French spiritualists call the subtle body the *Périsprit,* while in India the dreambody is the *Linga Shareirah.* For the Rosicrucians the dreambody is the "vital body."

A field of intensity around the body appears in the occultist's idea of the aura. Occultists hold that their "subtle body" gets its energy from the sun[15] and produces an aura around the real body. The aura is referred to as the "fine or etheric" body. According to occult tradition this aura may be controlled by the person initiated into the mysteries. The aura is supposed to have a radiation from the body between 1 inch and 100 feet.[16] It is a "field of force"[17] and is connected to a silvery form which can be seen by clairvoyants to leave the body at death.[18]

The dreambody's aura or field radiation often has colors associated with it. In the old religion of India, Jainism, the dreambody is called a "monad" or "life monad" which exists independently of time. The monad "pervades the whole organism, the body constitutes . . . its garb."[19] The monad's colors are dark (corresponding to mercilessness and cruelty), grey

[14]W.E. Butler, *How to Read the Aura,* p. 11.
[15]Ibid.
[16]Ibid.
[17]Ibid., p. 16.
[18]Ibid., p. 14.
[19]Heinrich Zimmer, *Philosophies of India,* p. 225.

(recklessness, thoughtlessness and uncontrollability), red (liveliness and passion) and clear white (purity).

Shamans, mediums and healers see the aura of the dreambody and can read the state of the personality from its color and form. The whitish glow or halo around the heads of Christ and God in pictures is an artist's intuition of subtle body "purity," clarity or wholeness. The existence of the aura-halo is implied by common expressions such as "He has a nice vibration, radiation or effect" or "It is nice to be around that person." I have sat in on healing sessions where a medium said that certain people have healing or destructive auras, corresponding, I believe, to their centeredness or repressed hostility, respectively.

Not only do modern seers and occultists see the soul as a field-like essence, but ancient doctrines also conceive of the inner human being as a radiant aura. In the *Bhagavad Gita,* for example, the dreambody is the "beholder," "thinker," "taster," "enjoyer" and all powerful one, the "he in the body who lights up the whole field."[20] The *Chandogya Upanishad* says that "orange, blue, yellow and red are not less in men's arteries than in the sun . . . As a long highway passes between two villages, one at either end, so the sun's rays pass between this world and the world beyond. They flow from the sun, enter into the arteries, flow back from the arteries and enter into the sun."[21] (See the arteries or *nadis* extending beyond the body in Fig. 7.)

It was thought that the sun's power entered the human body through the spleen (Fig. 8) and then spread throughout the body revitalizing the personality. This revitalization gives rise to "the undulating flow and rhythmically shimmering colour of the mental and astral fields."[22] The word *aura* is derived in fact from the Greek word *avra,* which means breeze and is supposedly related to the breezy nature of the astral fields.

Although the clairvoyant vision of mediums or religious seers has perceived the dreambody in many ways throughout history, there are some similarities. The dreambody is always a ghost-like essence. For example, the Karanga and Mashona peo-

[20]David V. Tansley, *Subtle Body, Essence and Shadow,* p. 18.
[21]Ibid.
[22]Ibid., p. 25.

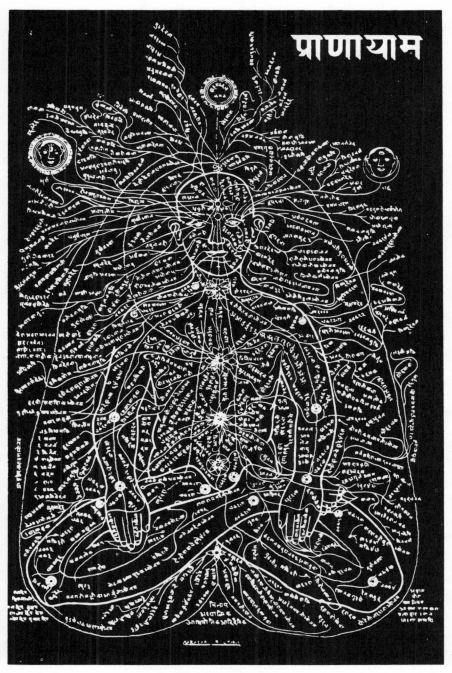

प्राणायाम

7. *The Subtle Arteries*

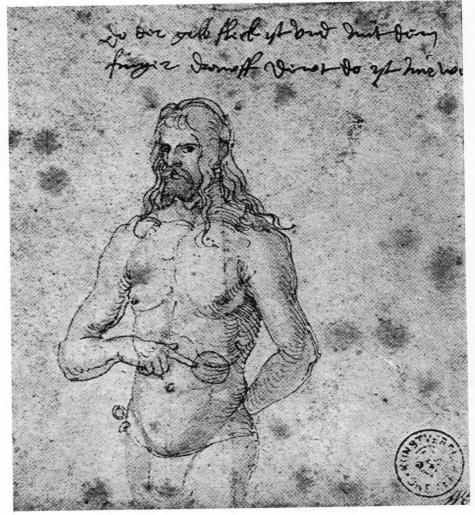

8. *The Sun-Absorbing Center as the Spleen*

ple of Rhodesia see the soul as an "invisible shadow" which leaves the body at death; their "mwega" is a "white darkness."[23] Europeans have had similar concepts. Paracelsus believed in an "invisible body" within the real form,[24] and the visionary Jacob Boehme saw the soul as an "inward man."[25] The early Greek philosopher Damascius perceived "radiant augoeides," or forms of radiance, in the human body. In his *Phaedrus,* Plato conceived of the soul as imprisoned in the body like "an oyster in the shell."[26]

In the Bible the true man is seen as a seed: "God giveth it a body . . . and to every seed his own body" (Corinthians 15:38). The Bible describes the highly evolved person as "wheels turning within wheels,"[27] and the real body containing this seed is seen as a temple or city. Man is the Holy City of Ezekiel. And Jesus said, "Destroy this temple and in three days I shall rise up again." The Jews built their tabernacles in the form of man. Likewise the Egyptian temple at Kernak and the temples in India are created according to the structure of the body.[28] In the *Upanishads,* the body is seen as the "city of Brahman," the Self or God.[29] The real body is conceived in Indian mythology not as a temple but as a god, the monkey Hanuman who contains Shiva and Parvati in the chest and heart area.[30] (See Fig. 9.)

Conceiving of the real body as a temple for the spirit seems relatively easy. However, the reader may find it difficult to accept the concept of the dreambody as a subtle essence, aura or radiation permeating and extending beyond the real body. Nonetheless, the psychologist must occasionally deal with out-of-body experiences. For example, the person who is not in the body is essentially not here. This person may need to be in another place, may require a dissociation from the present and may even gain a perspective on reality by really being "out of it." Other individuals may leave the body and discover that the personality extends, as Fig. 7 indicates, into the environment. For other people, such experiences are a preparation for death.

In some cases, visionary experiences occur during body work to form the first stages of actually acquiring a body. Many people are not aware of their physical bodies. Either they do not like them or must repress them because of their embarrass-

[23]Ibid., p. 21.   [24]Ibid., p. 5.   [25]Ibid.   [26]Ibid., p. 6.
[27]Ibid., p. 26.   [28]Ibid., p. 8.   [29]Ibid., p. 9.   [30]Ibid., p. 10.

9. *The Indian Monkey God, Hanuman*

ing pains or joys and unconsciously contribute to making themselves physically ill. Dreambody experiences are, for these persons, "para-sensations" of physical reality and predictions of the body to come. The therapist, surprised or frustrated by the seemingly psychic nature of some people's physical experiences, may see that the body itself often appears in the next step of development.

Don Juan's description of the dreambody as the double, or as "the warrior himself," seems to me an amazingly conscious understanding of body impulses and highly enlightened in comparison to the mediumistic visions of the dreambody such as the Kundalini snake, aura or glow. Don Juan stresses that the more a person is himself, the more the glow of the aura takes on the structure of the personality as dreambody awareness grows. Then the dreambody is more than a colorful field intensity or disturbing shadow. The complete person is simply himself. Double, field intensity or subtle body are merely descriptions useful only in the states preceding dreambody consciousness.

THE DREAMBODY AS A CHAKRA SYSTEM

In dreams, meditation, and drug experiences, the dreambody frequently appears as an out-of-body field intensity, as a total gestalt moving with relatively vague extremities in a sort of magnetic field. During normal states of consciousness when attention is turned to the real body, the dreambody appears in the form of total gestalts such as hunger, desire, fatigue and joy. But the dreambody can also appear as a localized pain or a spontaneous movement of the body.

Often body signals such as spasms, tics and illness arise in particular areas of the body and remain there. In these cases the dreambody seems to be located in the stomach, intestines, heart, skin, head, neck or back. In some bodies chronic problems travel from organ to organ, disappearing in one spot and reappearing in another. Attempts to heal these mercurial ailments seem to succeed temporarily but are followed by new ailments often more difficult to treat medically.

Although some people complain louder than others about body problems, no one I have met has been spared the mercurial behavior of the body, which occurs more or less regularly in everyone. Although we can learn a great deal about the general nature of the dreambody by studying the associations to body centers that arise in connection with specific practices, we cannot expect these associations to retain absolute validity for given individuals. In fact, I have found that in practice the existence, individuality and significance of particular body centers arising from illness, work, sports or meditation are rarely illuminated by knowledge of the archetypal centers. Because of our lack of personal body experience we tend to attach too much importance to the archetypal chakras of the East. Even gurus and yogis warn about trying to discover the chakras, claiming that personal experience reveals them in time. It is simply significant that archetypal body symbolism exists, is constellated by specific procedures and exposes certain nerve plexi which correspond to given psychic processes.

The various subtle body systems of the East and West remind me again of the particle concepts in field physics. The chakras themselves are defined in India as "wheels" or "vortex centers of energy."[31] They are like the elementary particles of physics which are high intensities or discontinuities in a quantum field. In fact, the essences of the chakras are called "elements," "tattwas" or "vibrations."[32] These tattwas have specific elemental characteristics. Specific chakras reveal certain elements of consciousness. When these centers open up in meditation, the body awakens to its potential vitality, sensation and consciousness. Simultaneously typical visions frequently occur.[33]

Just as Jung sees the psyche as a collection of complexes, each possessing an "energetic charge," "luminosity" and consciousness, so we are now discovering a dreambody picture consisting of energy vortices which possess archetypal experiences. In other words, the Jungian concept of the psyche may be applied to the dreambody. *The dreambody is a collection of energy vortices held together by the total personality.*

In psychological work, the complexes appear and disappear in cyclical fashion as development spirals toward the Self. In subtle physiology the energetic exchange between chakras is governed by the so-called "tattwic tides" which follow astrological or planetary influences. In other words, the particular

[31]Peter Rendel, *Introduction to the Chakras*, p. 17.
[32]Ibid., p. 19.
[33]See the autobiography of Swami Baba Muktananda, *The Play of Consciousness.*

body states and fantasies appearing at any given moment are personal manifestations of the periodic Tao, the changing collective unconscious, the field in which we live. Chakra theory indicates that *body states are synchronistically connected with the environment.*[34]

The idea of the synchronistic connection between the body and the universe is reflected in the early European theory of the body as a map of the universe.[35] The human being is a mirror of the field around him, and the structure of this field at any moment is given by the "constellation," the planets or archetypes of the time (Figs. 10 and 11). For early Europeans the world itself was God's body and man was seen at its center. This idea also appears in the Indian concept of man as god. The picture of man as a microcosmic image of the macrocosm appears in many places, such as China and Central America. From these different conceptions we see again that the dreambody is experienced as part of a living field.

There are cases which seem to support this conclusion. In any one area people often experience powerful physical symptoms spontaneously, synchronistically and apparently independently of one another at any given moment. I'll never forget

[34]Rendel, p. 22.
[35]Warren Kenton, *Astrology, The Celestial Mirror.*

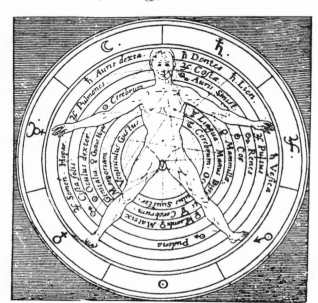

10. *Man and the Universe*

11. The Universe as Body of God

an experience I had years ago in a small mountain village in the Alps. There was a legend in that village that every time a mountain ghost came down from the rock wall about the village, everyone became ill. One night I awoke and thought that I saw a ghost in the small hut where I was staying. After quieting my fright—I had never seen a ghost before nor have I seen one since—I finally went to sleep. Next morning I met some peasants who excitedly reported that Skyscraper (a little peasant) had died during the night, that someone else had gotten pneumonia and others had become sick. It seemed to me that twelve sick persons in a town of twenty-five statistically spoke against mere chance!

Synchronicities are not dependent only on the Tao or spirit of an area but may occur between persons who are emotionally connected. In one outstanding case, a young woman developed intense pains in her breast at the same time her sister, in a distant place and unbeknown to anyone, visited her physician and received a diagnosis of breast cancer. Shortly thereafter, the first woman also developed cancer in the same breast as the sister and both women died consequently of the same problem.

There is practical significance in knowing that body synchronicities exist. Strong, spontaneous, unusual symptoms may be connected with environmental situations. Hence, getting oneself in order, making oneself more comfortable, letting out certain pressures or living certain feelings may have a relieving effect on others, whether or not one's problems are worked out in public.[36]

Just as the body was conceived in Europe as a manifestation of the universe, so particular parts of the body were supposed to be governed by given planets. We see in Fig. 12, for example, how the solar plexus area is governed by Leo, sign of the summer sun, passion and aggression. This aspect of the stomach or solar plexus area is also found in the Indian conception of the area, the so-called *manipura,* center of passion, fire and even destructiveness. In Fig. 13, we see a 15th century Indian astrological body picture in which a serpent is associated with the genitals, according to their planetary system. This image corresponds to the Kundalini, the coiled serpent at rest in the base of the spine in Indian subtle body theory.

The idea that planets or archetypes symbolize experiences, fantasies and sensations connected to particular body locations is also found in China, where special gods and "governing dignitaries" are attributed to particular body centers.[37] The Chinese thought that illness occurred when these gods wandered out of the body and returned to their astrological abodes in the universe. This theory corresponds to the shamanistic idea that illness comes from a loss of soul. In psychological terminology we speak of persons who are too much in their heads, who are out of their bodies, who are depressed, lonely or in creative moods.

The number of body centers varies according to given cultures just as it does among individuals. In Western occult tradition there are five body centers located on the spinal axis

[36]This, of course, is the essence of Richard Wilhelm's "rainmaker story," related by Jung in *CW,* Vol. 14, p. 419, fn. 211.
[37]R. Homann, *Die wichtigsten Körpergottheiten im Huan-t'ing Ching.*

12. *Planets in the Body*

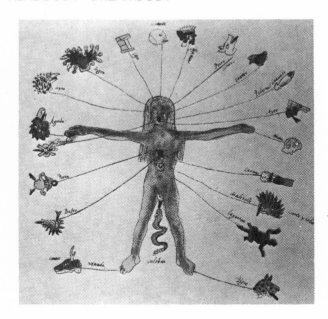

13. *Aztec Body Astrology*

through which energy from the earth and sun distributes itself in the body.[38] Eastern subtle body pictures contain five, six or seven chakras depending on whether Indian, Tibetan, Chinese, Buddhist or Hindu formulations are used. In the West the centers are above the head, in the throat, heart, sexual area and beneath the feet. In the typical Eastern Indian portrait, the centers are located above the head, between the eyes, in the heart, solar plexus, spleen and sacral region and in the base of the spine (Fig. 14).[39] Apparently the Kyushas, or seven body centers of the Japanese martial arts, are derivatives of Indian subtle body theories.[40]

The relationship between the different subtle body centers and nerve plexi, or nerve junctions of the real body, may be seen by comparing Figs. 14 and 15. This relationship often causes theoretical arguments. Are dreambody sensations "caused" by the real body? Or is the occultist thesis correct that the real body results from the descent of the spirit into matter?

Both arguments have certain validity and application. The first explains why mechanical and chemical changes in certain

[38]Butler, *How To Read the Aura,* p. 25.
[39]Swami Baba Muktananda, *The Play of Consciousness,* p. 119.
[40]John Mumford, *Psychosomatic Yoga,* p. 46.

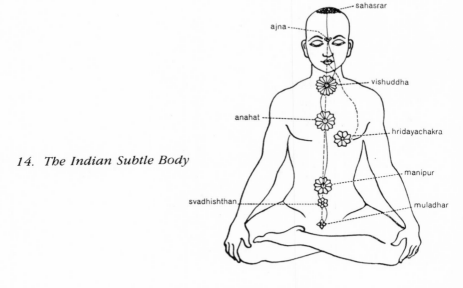

14. The Indian Subtle Body

body areas appear to affect dreams, while the second conception supports the psychologist's observation that changes in attitude apparently alter body experience. Both types of causal
thinking are useful analogues of what may actually be happening, but both are limited rational explanations. An empirical
understanding of the relationship between the real body and
the subtle body is simply that they are both two aspects of one
thing—the dreambody.

Now, for the sake of completeness, I would like to review
some of the characteristics attributed to the chakras and add my
own practical observations about these body centers.[41]

The chakra at the base of the Indian subtle body system is
called the *Muladhara* or the "root support," corresponding to
the gonads and sexual function of the real body. Malfunctions
in this area are related to impotence, nymphomania and frigid-
ity.[42] In this center is the elephant (Fig. 16), India's symbol of
domesticated energy roughly equivalent to the significance we
in the West attribute to the horse. In my experience with this

[41]For a complete presentation of the chakras, see Werner Bohm, *Chakras*. For
a classical presentation of the body centers, see Arthur Avalon, *The Serpent
Power*.
[42]Mumford, p. 43.

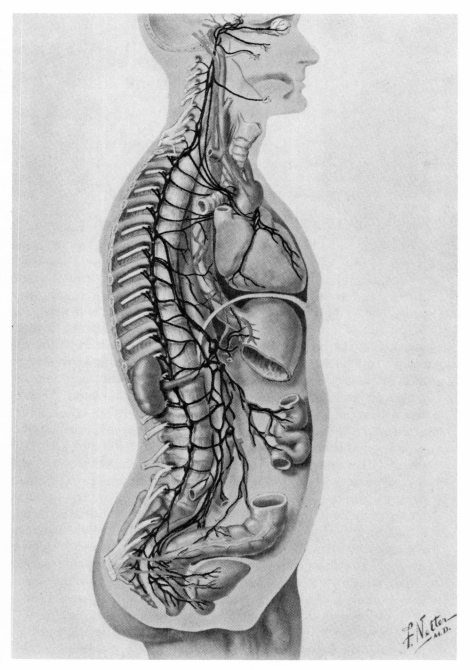

15. Nerve Plexi

*16. Muladhara or
    Base Chakra*

center, troubles with the sexual organs and urinary function are often connected to overly domesticated, strictly trained compulsiveness. This area is the first one to become conscious in life. Toilet training domesticates the horse, so to speak. Cramping in the genital area is therefore frequently related to the inability to let go in public life. One restricts the inner animal or child who defecates and urinates at will and who exercises no control over himself. Inhibited creativity is also related to functional disorders in the genital area.

The *Swadhistana* chakra corresponds to sensations of the kidneys and adrenals. Makara the whale lives here (Fig. 17). The Swadhistana is the fluid center and symbolizes the unconscious for us, since this chakra lies just beyond the center of civilization, the Muladhara. The fluid chakra is really only the first experience or level of the unconscious and carries the terrifying whale in it because first experiences of the non-ego normally overwhelm the domesticated focus. The more one holds to normal consciousness, the more the fish become a negative whale which devours. Then the unconscious becomes a negative mother, the body becomes a tyrannical terror threatening a dry consciousness, holding to chronological time.

Physiological problems in this area include uterine trouble, prostate difficulties, bladder and kidney trouble, as well as general lack of fluidity experienced in connection with heat pros-

*17. Swadisthana or
Sacral Chakra*

trations and arthritis.[43] In my experience, people with troubles
in this area feel that they are hemmed in by social obligations.

The *Manipura* lies in the solar plexus area (Fig. 18).[44] The
"lustrous gem," as the center is called, contains the ram, symbol of Agni, god of fire, and is known as "second mind." Here
also is Maras, instinct of impulsiveness and violence. This is the
area of animal wisdom or "gut knowledge" where many asser-
tive reactions are repressed and turned into aggressiveness and
anger. Stomach cramps, ulcers, "heartburn," diabetes and
cancer are related to this area.

The violence associated with the *Manipura* corresponds to
the stomach area as center of food dissolution and destruction.
In my experience, the stomach area becomes the center for unmitigated violence when its wisdom or signals are unheard.
This area reacts when the "mind" directs and ignores the body.
The split between the ego and stomach wisdom appears from
this area in the form of moans, groans and sporadic deep
breaths. The diaphragm which controls breathing lies just
above the stomach and just beneath the lungs.

The heart area is called the *Anahata,* place of the "unstruck
sound," where the yogi says God reaches down to man.[45] Jung

[43]Ibid.
[44]See Bohm, *Chakras*.
[45]Zimmer, *Philosophies of India,* p. 584.

18. Manipuraka or Solar Plexus Chakra

interprets the gazelle who lives in this area (Fig. 19)[46] as a symbol of psychosomatic problems because of the gazelle's lightness and swiftness.[47] The cardiac area is the source of functional problems which medicine calls hypochondria (hypo = under, chondria = chest bone). Here the heart is felt to skip beats or to cramp, stop, die or become overexcited. Noise arises from this area in association with the beating heart and gives rise to the concept of the "unstruck sound" in this area. Actually the "unstruckness" means that the sound seems to come from nowhere. The unconscious reaches down into conscious life and may be heard and controlled in this area through the breath. Yogis are supposed to be able to control their heart rate. In my experience the heartbeat is often associated with naive sentimentality. When fantasies related to heart motions are worked through, then one cleans out the heart center, and objective feelings often experienced as "god's feelings" arise from the heart.

The *Vishuddha* is located in the throat plexus (Fig. 20).[48] This is the "purification center," experienced as ether, air, wind and a door that swings back and forth without cause.[49] Typical problems associated by many authors with this area are "de-

---

[46]See Bohm, *Chakras.*
[47]C. G. Jung, "Psychological Commentary on Kundalini Yoga."
[48]Bohm, *Chakras.*
[49]Shunryu Suzuki, *Zen Mind, Beginner's Mind,* p. 13.

19. Anahata or Heart Chakra

20. Vishuddha or Throat Chakra

pression and speech trouble."[50] The voice is easily disturbed by the persona or social mask since the *natural* sounds of the voice do not often conform to the effect one wants to create. The voice can also be used to manipulate others. This is a center of purification because the voice may be easily cleansed of false behavior. Then the heart, stomach and genital area may manifest themselves through the voice of feeling, violence or sensuousness.

[50]Mumford, *Psychosomatic Yoga.*

The *Ajna* center, between the eyes, corresponds to the pituitary gland and is the seat of "thinking," worry and anxiety (Fig. 21).[51] Here is where the sense of time as the flow of mental images and internal dialogue arises. But this is also the center of command (in Indian theory) where one can or must learn to control the flow of images, cancel out time and experience freedom by emptying the mind. The *Ajna* is the point where time and timelessness come together. Shakti with Shiva. *Ajna* is the god center containing the winged seed. The seed with wings indicates that when thoughts are stopped—when the anima, animus or shadow is quieted through integration (or repression)—inspirations seem to come from nowhere, from the Self.

The *Sahasrara,* "lotus of the 1000 petals," is Brahman, experience of oneness, timelessness and formlessness at the top of the head, corresponding to the pineal gland (Fig. 22) and the brain cells.[52] The *Kundalini* arises here and creates the magical *Siddhas* or parapsychological phenomena. At this point, experience leaves the personal realm and connects to the universe. Here the mythical marriage, the *unus mundus,* the "I am" or god experience occurs. This point is often turned on by heat or blood pulsations at the top of the skull. The body seems to press and search for recognition and understanding here. Men-

[51]Bohm, *Chakras.*
[52]Mumford, *Psychosomatic Yoga.*

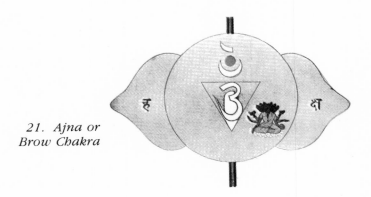

21. Ajna or Brow Chakra

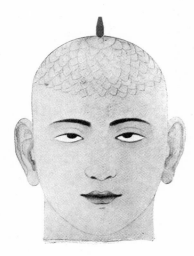

22. Sahasrara

tal stimulation, or unconscious material straining for meaning and consciousness, frequently creates pressure in the *Sahasrara*. Meditators frequently experience the blood streaming out of their head into the arteries of the universe. Excess pressure in this area may therefore also be related to mundane, limited attitudes.

The mysterious transformation of experience into knowledge, or matter into psyche, occurring at the top of the head is symbolized in Kundalini yoga by the serpent being carried off by the eagle, Guarda. These images express the soul's transit out of the body after having become conscious through body experience. The Chinese express this transformation in terms of the birth of the so-called Immortal Fetus (Fig. 23) which, through body alchemy, becomes conscious and independent of the body as one realizes previous births.[53] What the mind observes as the discovery of roots or meaning, the body experiences as liberation from itself and from time and space (Figs. 24 and 25).

A crucial element in the Eastern experience of oneself as an immortal being is the fact that this achievement occurs through working on the body, in contrast to Western occult so-called subtle body experiences which frequently happen independently of the body. The West attempts to create immortality and reach heaven mainly through good works, and more

[53]Lu K'uan Yü, *Taoist Yoga*.

圖 胎 道

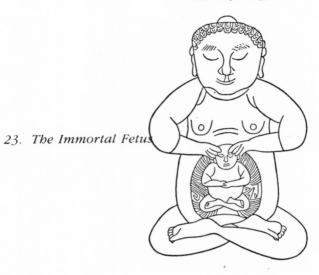

23. *The Immortal Fetus*

圖 胎 出

24. *Birth of the Self*

25. Being Everywhere

recently through psychological growth and self-knowledge. Our tendency to skip the body itself partially accounts for our compulsive preoccupation with material security and physical health. It is as if we skipped stages 1 through 7 in order to rush into stage 8 of life. But if the body is not integrated into self-knowledge, one becomes obsessed with its well-being. Psychological growth without body consciousness appears like a tree without roots.

Cultures are like individuals insofar as their consciousness is located in particular areas of the body. Generally speaking, the West is a "head tripper" and is bound to *Ajna,* between the eyes, center of command. We manipulate our bodies and environments with our ideas, barely realizing that we are being controlled by an unmitigated flow of internal dialogue and unconsciousness. This is why much of our psychology is devoted to uprooting and understanding the personal shadow, the human figures in dreams, the stuff which keeps our world going. We feel like the drivers, but we also experience ourselves as driven by time. The flow of mental images possesses us. We

do not hear the falseness of the voice, the ridiculous sentimentality of the heart or the aggression of the stomach.

India, in aiming at the *Sahasrara* or nirvana chakra, subtly
devaluates the *Muladhara* or lowest chakra corresponding
to the base materiality of domesticated life. Hence, India
suffers from earthly problems. Her command of everyday life is
almost as archaic as the Western commander's relationship to
spirituality.

The American Indian tends to live in the stomach or solar
plexus area, which means that he follows his gut reactions and
his animal intelligence but has not developed the differentiated
feelings of the heart or the logical thinking of the head's command center. The ancient Greeks also attributed the mind or
consciousness to the solar plexus area, as we can still see in the
word *phren* which means both diaphragm and mind (e.g.,
schizophrenia means split mind).

The Eastern subtle body theories instruct us about the nerve
centers experienced by consciousness and also present us with
dynamic structures of how these centers are connected.

In India, the imaginary channels connecting the body centers
are called *nadis*. These *nadis* carry prana or energy, symbolized by the Kundalini. When the serpent is aroused its energy
flows along the Ida or Pingala, the moon or sun circuits, corresponding to quiet or passionate energies. Directing the Kundalini through these channels is achieved through breathing
and concentration methods. When balance is achieved, energy
flows through a third circuit which lies in between the Ida and
Pingala, the so-called *Shushuma* (Fig. 43, Chapter 4).

The paths that body energy take are defined by various cultures in different ways; yet the basic positive/ negative polarity
is universal.

The Chinese and Tibetan subtle body pictures (Figs. 26 and
27) portray not two or three energy passages but twelve or
more "meridians" which pass throughout the body.[54] The concept of body centers plays a minor role in these conceptions
and is replaced by the existence of special points on the meridians from which energy may be added or withdrawn (in acupuncture or bloodletting) according to whether energy is

[54]Rinpoche Rechung, *Tibetan Medicine.*

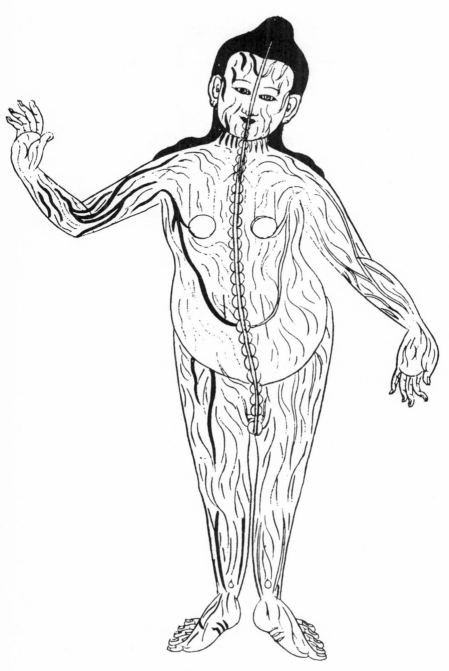

26. *Tibetan Subtle Body*

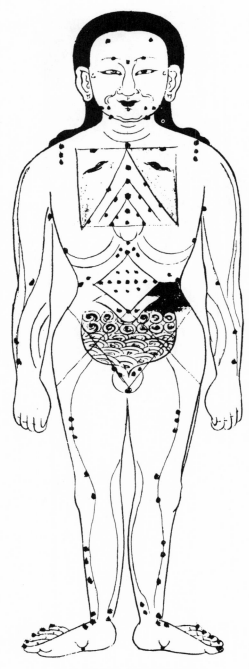

27. *Chinese Subtle Body*

blocked, leaking or overloading a given yin or yang circuit (Fig. 28).[55] In Taoist ritual, the body is pictured as a vessel for the alchemical process, and certain centers or "gates" are found in the stomach, back and neck region where transformation processes of the *prima materia* take place (Fig. 29).

While the flow lines of the meridian system (Figs. 26 and 27) correspond to the *li*, "law" or "structure" of the Tao flowing through the body,[56] the alchemical circulation of vitality (Fig. 29) arises in connection with active imagination on the body done in conjunction with deep breathing techniques. Physiological imaginations appear, with the sensations of the cold breath passing through the nostrils going into the lungs and beyond and also with the experience of the heartbeat in the various arteries of the body. People with absolutely no knowledge whatsoever of Indian or Chinese body theories spontaneously see, in meditation, silver and red channels in their bodies and special points on the body surfaces corresponding to acupuncture spots. Like the *asanas* of hatha yoga, the imaginary circuitry, points and body centers of the subtle body system seem to be archetypal experiences arising in conjunction with particular exercises and breathing techniques.

CONCLUSION

Dreambody properties have been discussed in this chapter in terms of death experiences, scientific field concepts, Taoism, doubles, astral bodies, auras, dance, subtle body centers and shamanistic ideas. The common picture of the dreambody emerging from these properties is a highly energic field intensity, that is, a patterned experience without definite spatial or temporal dimensions.

In practice the exact nature of the dreambody appears in reference to specific conditions. For example, if one is asleep the dreambody appears as dream images. A materialistic culture imagines glorified body images of the dreambody. The dancer experiences the dreambody as the creative impulse behind movement. The meditator sees the dreambody as an internal subtle body structure with specific centers. Someone in a mediumistic mood or intense body experience apprehends the

[55]F.M. Houston, *The Healing Benefits of Acupressure,* p. 15.
[56]Needham translation of *li* in Capra, *The Tao of Physics,* p. 306.

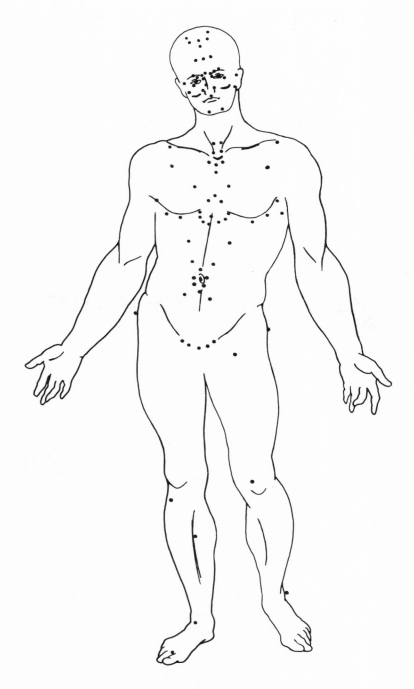

28. Acupuncture Points

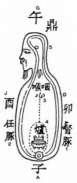

Figure 1 The four cardinal points: A bottom, G top, D back, J front 1 Channel of control (tu mo) 2 channel of function (jen mo) 3 heart 4 stove 5 precious cauldron (See also figure 8, p. 124)

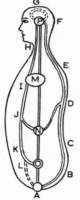

The channel of control (*tu mo*)
A B C D E F:
A (tzu *cardinal point North*—the mortal gate (sheng szu ch'iao)
B (ch'uo) intermediate point
C (yin) intermediate point
D (mao) *cardinal point East, wood* (cleansing)
E (ch'en) intermediate point
F (szu) intermediate point
The channel of function (jen mo)
G H I J K L :
G (wu) *cardinal point South*—the brain (ni wan)
H (wei) intermediate point
I (shen) intermediate point
J (yu) *cardinal point West, metal* (purifying)
K (shu) intermediate point
L (hai) intermediate point
The thrusting channel (ch'ung mo)
M N O A :
M (li) the heart—house of fire
N (chung t'u) the central earth, the solar plexus (chiang kung)
O (k'an) the lower tan t'ien— house of water
P The centre of the brain(tsu ch'iao)
The channels of control, function and thrusting.

The heel and trunk channels. 1 the heel channel (tung chung) from the heels to the brain. 2 the trunk channel (tung ti) from the lower abdomen to the brain.

29. *Alchemical Channels*

dreambody as a fantasy or aura. The sick person knows the dreambody as the symptoms of illness while the dying person knows the dreambody as an out-of-body experience which normally occurs only in hypometabolic conditions (where breathing and heart rate are depressed).

In practice, work on the dreambody depends on its mode of expression. Sometimes it appears as the psyche in dream form, sometimes as matter in body motions; sometimes as synchronicities or accidents. In any given session dreambody processes oscillate between psyche and matter.

Practical experience has created a specific personal conception of the dreambody for me. Before bodywork or psychological understanding, the dreambody appears to me like Shiva and Parvati in Fig. 9, that is, as a hidden reality unknown to the unconscious ape carrying it. Before dreambody work, the real body seems to me like a potential temple which is unaware of the gods it is carrying. After body work and dream study, the differentiation between the dreambody and the real body is less defined because the two merge, creating the total personality. The real body begins to glow as the dreambody assumes the appearance of the real living person.

Chapter 3
THE DREAMBODY
IN FAIRY TALES

If we use symbols to examine physiological processes, we can choose to study many separate dreams or we can study their generalization in the form of fairy tales.[1] Far from being just stories for children, these tales genuinely express the unconscious. Their symbols serve to delineate the structure of psychic process such as negative mother feelings (the Witch), the principles of consciousness (the King), the Self (the Fool), and the instincts (the Serpent). Of course, archetypes such as the Witch or King may not appear as such in dreams but may take on the personal associations of the dreamer. Thus fairy tales can generalize personal experiences.

This chapter shows that fairy tales, which are widely accepted as important in the study of psychological processes, are also essential in the study of the body. We first look at fairy tales and myths that involve illness and healing because disturbances in health are normally the first conscious indication of the dreambody's existence. Naturally, some people can experience their dreambodies without having to become ill. In fact, awareness of body sensations and their relationships to dreams may even prevent illness.

THE SPIRIT IN THE BOTTLE
One of my own dreams first indicated to me the importance of mythical processes in the investigation of the dreambody. In the dream I was writing a paper on the connection between psychology and physiology, and the theme turned out to be the god Mer-

[1]Marie-Louise von Franz, *Introduction to the Psychology of Fairy Tales*, pp. 1, 2.

cury. The only association to Mercury that occurred to me was
Jung's paper, "The Spirit Mercurius,"[2] which discusses Grimm's
fairy tale "The Spirit in the Bottle."[3] Here is my version of the
story:

> Once there was a poor woodcutter who could not afford to send
> his son through the higher schools. So when there was no longer
> any money, the son had to come home from school and help his
> father in the forest. One day during a midday break, the boy was
> wandering through the woods and suddenly heard a voice coming
> from a great oak.
>
> "Let me out!" called the voice.
>
> The young man dug among the roots of the tree and found a
> bottle from which the voice was coming. He opened it and out
> came a spirit which grew to one-half the height of the tree.
>
> "I am the great spirit Mercurius," said the monster, "and I will
> avenge my imprisonment by strangling you."
>
> But the young man thought quickly and told the spirit that its
> greatness must be tested. "Show your powers by getting back into
> the bottle," he said. The spirit reentered and the boy put the cork
> back into the bottle, locking him up. The spirit immediately prom-
> ised to give the boy rewards if he would let him out again. When
> the boy released him, the spirit gave him a rag. One side of the rag
> could turn metal to silver, and the other side could heal any
> wound.
>
> The boy made a wound on a tree with his axe and tested the rag.
> The tree healed immediately. The father thought the boy was a
> blockhead to want to quit work in the middle of the day, but when
> the boy showed him that he could turn the axe to silver, the father
> accepted him, and the boy became a rich and famous doctor.

When I began to study this fairy tale, I discovered that Mercury, whom Jung called "god of the unconscious," was also the
god of the body. But I had many questions: Why was body experience symbolized by Mercury? What was Mercury, a body
experience, doing in a bottle? I had often seen how individuals
can imagine or experience "something" bottled up inside themselves—in the lungs, the stomach—but in the fairy tale, Mercury
was bottled up at the base of a tree. Why?

[2]C. G. Jung, "The Spirit Mercurius," *CW,* Vol. 13.
[3]*Grimm's Fairy Tales,* no. 99.

Mercury

Mercury was alchemy's basic substance which had to be caught, refined, and cooked until it turned into a magical substance called the "panacea."[4] Mercury was the *prima materia*, which if stewed and bottled was supposed to transform into great medicine, the pill for immortality, or the finest metal, such as silver or gold. Mercury's liquid volatility made it the source of unending projections, which Jung sifted through before discovering that Mercury was indeed the god of the unconscious.[5] He was the spirit behind dreams, fantasies, and synchronicities. He was the living water, the magical trickster who could adapt himself to any situation, the king of liars and thieves. In dreams he may appear as the fool, the dumbling, wise old man, the wise old woman, the elf, the magician, and the stag.[6] He symbolizes elusive creativity which produces all psychic material.

But although Mercury is a central concept in psychology, his relationship to physiology is less talked about and less known. In a Chinese text, *Taoist Yoga,* the spirit Mercury appears in connection with meditation. Taoist yoga is described as "an ancient science which teaches the stopping of the flow of generative force inherent in every man so that instead of being discharged to procreate offspring or to waste away, it is retained in the body for purification and transmutation . . . to restore the original spirit which existed before the world came into being. . . ."[7] This is basically a procedure for bringing involuntary spontaneous actions under conscious control. The Taoists considered alchemy as the science or art of meditating upon the body in order to transform the body itself into a magical substance. Mercury was not simply a chemical substance to the Taoists; he was understood as a body experience. They defined Mercury in terms of the word *spirit,* and spirit as "the divine in man or his immortal nature which derives from the purification of vitality. . . ."[8]

[4]A popular account of alchemy can be found in Stanislaus Klossowski de Rola's *The Secret of Alchemy.*
[5]C.G. Jung, "The Spirit Mercurius."
[6]Ibid.
[7]Lu K'uan Yü, *Taoist Yoga: Alchemy and Immortality,* p. 177.
[8]Ibid., p. 196.

For the Taoists *vitality* was apparently understood as spontaneous impulses—the drives, forces and creations we refer to as physical motions and the act of thinking. By observing and becoming aware of unconscious instinctive actions, the alchemist purified his nature and realized Mercury, the spirit, which "leads to the realization of the essential nature and vitality to eternal life which are the aim of Taoist Alchemy."[9] Thus the goal is to realize the transcendental nature of instinctive acts. "Essential nature" and "eternal life" are meditation experiences for the alchemist and refer to direct knowledge of the causeless, spontaneous spark behind action. If one can contact this spark, then *wu wei,* or effortless existence, timelessness, and hence a sense of immortality result.

India's Tantric and Kundalini yoga also attempt to transform the real body by the achievement of a high degree of awareness and control of body energy. The Indian symbol for this energy, *Kundalini,* is a spirit buried in the earth, asleep and waiting to be awakened and purified. Kundalini is a serpent, one of Mercury's typical forms in European alchemy. Lying dormant in the base of the spine, the Kundalini symbolizes pulsatile, vibrant, energetic charges which may awaken either spontaneously or through Hatha yoga exercises and breathing meditation. When awakened, the Kundalini must be guided through the various body centers, or *chakras,* which she in turn energizes.[10]

In Tantric yoga Mercury appears as the pleasure principle. *Shakti,* or Kundalini, is aroused through ritualized excitation of all the senses. The *tantrika* consciously participates in forbidden pleasures such as extramarital sex, contact with partners of lower caste, and eating meat,[11] in order to awaken shakti.

In Chinese alchemy Mercury appears variously as an alchemical substance, as sexuality, as "doing" creativity and body energy, but in Taoist and Kundalini yogas, the god appears as a feminine spirit. In Siddha yoga she takes on other characteristics. Here the same god is called Shakti, and worshipped as the origin of pain, diseases, tingling, tremor, strange tastes, sudden visions, weird noises, and wild dreams.[12] The Siddha yogi uses

[9]Ibid.
[10]Philip Rawson, *Tantra: The Indian Cult of Ecstasy.* The Chinese subtle body image appears in Philip Rawson and Laszlo Legeza, *Tao: The Chinese Philosophy of Time and Change,* p. 29.
[11]Rawson, *Tantra: The Indian Cult of Ecstasy,* p. 19.
[12]Swami Baba Muktananda, *The Play of Consciousness.*

simple concentration on breathing to develop a relationship to "her will" and to experience some of these manifestations.

The Siddha yogi worships spontaneous phenomena that occur during meditation, and transforms them through devotion and conversation. The Buddhist and Zen Buddhist meditators, however, experience body mercuriality as mental or physical perturbations which must be merely tolerated until they disappear into nothingness and enlightenment by themselves.[13]

The spirit caught in the bottle in our fairy tale has now acquired psycho-physical dimensions. Psychologically, Mercury appears as the spirit of dreams, visions, and spontaneous creativity. Physiologically, he is found in the body in the form of sexual impulses, compulsions and spontaneous body motions such as tics, itches, pain, finger motions, headaches and diseases.

Amplifying Mercury's nature with the help of alchemy, yoga, and meditation shows that the god of the unconscious is also god of the body, symbolizing uncontrolled psychic and physical energy. Mercury is the basic element in alchemical experiments, in body alchemy, and in yoga's search for immortality and pure spirituality. Whether we work on visions, dreams, synchronicities, body spasms or diseases, we are dealing with one and the same dreambody mercuriality. Body work and dream analysis share one characteristic in common: They both try to locate Mercury, observe his action in fantasies and body signals, meditate upon his nature, and associate and amplify his actions until they transform into an immortal substance, that is, individuation of the true human being.[14]

Trees

According to Teutonic mythology, Wotan created the first humans from the trunks of dead trees. Man was called the ash tree and woman the vine.[15] Celtic myths tell how human beings may be transformed into trees and then back again into humans.[16] The oak itself was used by the Druids and by the

[13]Joseph Goldstein, *The Experience of Insight: A Natural Unfolding.*
[14]C. G. Jung (*CW,* Vol. 11, pp. 520ff.) describes individuation symbolism in the different yogas.
[15]*New Larousse Encyclopedia of Mythology,* p. 249.
[16]W. B. Crow, *The Occult Properties of Herbs,* p. 56.

ancient Greeks as a semi-human, semi-divine oracle.[17] It was the center of the ancient and little known Druid religion. Remnants of Celtic tree cults in modern thinking can be found in Tolkien's *Lord of the Rings* where Ents, or tree-people, appear.[18]

The tree always has a spirit. For example, the tree of knowledge of good and evil is linked to the devilish serpent. In Siberia, a tree spirit tells a hero to take water from the tree's roots to heal wounds.[19] In European alchemy, Mercury, healer and messenger of the gods, is pictured at the center of a tree carrying his magical staff and flanked by two snakes.[20] (See Fig. 30.) This Mercury was also called the philosophical Mercury and the *aqua permanens* which was the origin of the tree's life.[21]

[17]Lewis Spence, *The History and Origins of Druidism,* pp. 12, 77–78.
[18]J. R. R. Tolkien, *Lord of the Rings.*
[19]Roger Cook, *The Tree of Life, Symbol of the Center.*
[20]Ibid., p. 112.
[21]Ibid.

30. Mercury in the Tree

After studying the tree's symbolism and comparing it to the spontaneous pictures of his patients, Jung described the tree as a symbol of individuation. He showed how the roots represented unconscious material, the trunk conscious realization, and the crown of the tree the goals of life and individuation.[22] The tree spirit is thus a structure of growth, a manifestation of mercurial life and of healing.

In Kundalini yoga the tree represents the spine or nervous system, the central axis of the universe which carries the serpent, or the Kundalini, to the crown, the top chakra in the head where the mythical eagle Guarda carries the serpent off into the air. This flight symbolizes the powerful visions that occur when the meditator has constellated the unconscious through deep inner focus.[23] In Kundalini yoga the tree thus represents the structure traced by body energy as sensations that occur in the various locations that coincide with the Kundalini's journey.

The practitioner of Tantric yoga also sees the tree as a map of body energy: "The human body is like a rootless tree and relies solely on the breath as root and branches."[24] Or according to an authority on Tantric yoga,

Indian tradition has always visualized the human body as growing like a plant from the ground of the beyond, the Supreme Brahman, the Truth [see Fig. 31]. And just as the vital juices of a plant are carried up and outwards from the root through the channels and veins, so are the creative energies in the human body. Only the root of the human plant is not below, but above, beyond the top of the skull over the spine. The nourishing and bewildering energy flows in from beyond at that point. After spreading along through the body's channels it flows to the outermost tips of the senses, and even further out, to project the space around it which each body believes it inhabits. The pattern of veins and channels which compose this system is called the subtle body and is the basis of all Tantric worship and yoga.[25]

[22]C.G. Jung, "The Philosophical Tree," *CW*, Vol. 13.
[23]Cook, *The Tree of Life*, p. 25.
[24]Lu K'uan Yü, *Taoist Yoga*, p. 27.
[25]Rawson, *Tantra*, pp. 20–21. Indian poets and mystics consistently use the tree to represent the body. See, for example, Mircea Eliade, *Yoga: Immortality and Freedom*, p. 251.

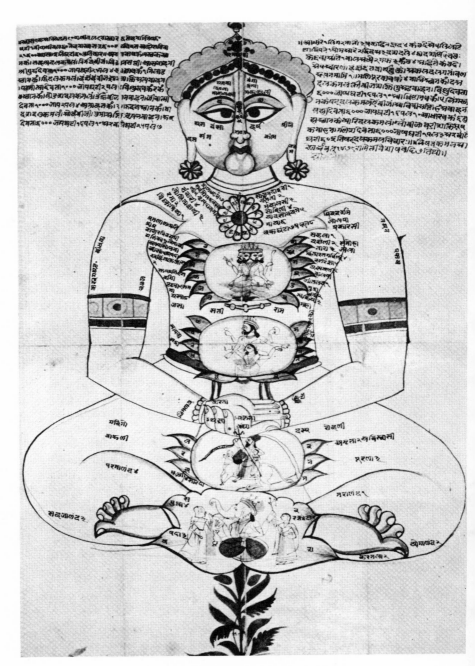

31. The Indian Subtle Body

Just as there is no complete agreement about the exact nature of the subtle body in the East,[26] so there seems to be no single dreambody image that appears to the various Western meditators whose body visions I have examined. The dreambody is an *individual* experience with some collective elements. Thus the tree symbolizes the experience of the dreambody, manifesting itself in vegetative physiological sensations. But the tree is only one manifestation of the dreambody. Mercury, the spirit of this body, may be located anywhere in this tree or, as our tale tells us, may even leave the tree area. When the spirit leaves the tree, visions, dreams, and out-of-body experiences occur.[27] When Mercury flows in the tree, the dreambody appears in terms of a real body.

Roots of Trees

The lowest chakra in Indian subtle body symbolism is called the *Muladhara,* which literally means roots or root support. This center is found at the base of the spine, the root of the 27,000 nadis of the subtle body, and is pictured as a pot or vessel containing the sleeping Kundalini or the seed. One finds the white elephant symbolizing earthy heaviness in the root chakra.[28]

Jung interpreted the Muladhara as follows:

> You see *Muladhara* is a whole world, each *chakra* is a whole world. Perhaps you remember the picture which a patient made of herself, entangled in the roots of the tree, and stretching her arms up towards the light above.[29] Now where was that woman when she was entangled in the roots? In what condition would that be in reality?
>
> The Self is then asleep, and in what stage is the Self asleep and the ego conscious? *Here,* of course, in this conscious world

[26]Lu K'uan Yü, *Taoist Yoga,* Foreword, p. xviii: "When they [the readers] have made real progress in their practice of Taoist yoga, they will automatically know where in the body these psychic centers really are, for the latter usually feel warm when the inner fire passes through them during its circulation in the microcosmic orbit. It is harmful to pinpoint places in the body . . . since it hinders the course of the inner fire."

[27]Robert A. Monroe describes many out-of-the-body or astral body experiences in his *Journeys Out of the Body.*

[28]Werner Bohm, *Chakras,* pp. 64, 65.

[29]See Jung's "Commentary on the 'Secret of the Golden Flower,'" *CW,* Vol. 13.

where we are all reasonable and respectable people, adapted individuals, as one says. Everything runs smoothly; we are normal
citizens of a certain state; we have appointments; we are under
certain obligations and cannot run away easily without getting
neurotic; we have to look after our duties. So we are all in the
roots, we are upon our root-support . . . We are entangled in
our roots right in this world—when we buy our tickets from the
street-car conductor, or for the theatre, or have lunch, or pay
the waiter—that is reality as we touch it. And then the Self is
asleep, which means that all things concerning the Gods are
asleep.[30]

The roots in our fairy tale symbolize psychological and physiological processes. The white elephant in the Muladhara is
roughly equivalent to the horse in our culture as a basic means
of transportation.[31] Modern elephants and horses would thus
be bicycles, motorcycles, cars, buses and trucks. All of these images are elephants in the Muladhara, i.e., symbols of the ordinary body, the unaware carrier of the spirit and the subtle
body. Hence, dreams about horses and vehicles of locomotion
commonly refer to the actual machine in which we are located.

Thus, the roots of the tree, the Muladhara, have psychophysical significance. The psychic manifestations of Mercury in the
roots for someone who is living mentally in the Muladhara
would be dreams, visions, and synchronicities. Such psychic
creations are signs in the ordinary world that though the "gods
are asleep" they are stirring. Physiologically, the Muladhara is
the ordinary body which is not yet awakened, developed, or
sensitive to the soul. *The roots are the points in space or time
where the soul manifests in the body.* The Muladhara is
therefore not only the root of the spine but the boundary between the soul and the body, where the dreambody manifests
in matter. In a synchronicity, the Muladhara would be represented by the physical objects whose behavior mirrors dreams.
In illness the Muladhara is the body location where Mercury appears in terms of symptoms. Hence, the roots (or Muladhara)
refer to the physical location of body symptoms, diseases, unpredictable motions and tics, sexuality, scratching, restlessness,
spasms, pains and excitement.

[30]C.G. Jung, "Psychological Commentary on Kundalini Yoga."
[31]Ibid.

The Bottle

"Root" manifestations of the dreambody are the starting point of individuation whether they are looked at as dreams or body signals. Jung pointed out that the glass bottle in our tale represents not only a natural bottling up in the roots, but also a human or conscious construction which bottles up Mercury.[32]

If we recall that this fairy tale originated when modern science was just beginning and alchemy was still in full swing in Europe, then we may consider that the bottle refers to the work of the alchemists, who literally caught mercury, bottled it up, put it in their "philosophical egg," as their vessel was called, and transformed it into another substance. Translated into psychological terms, this bottling refers to a mechanical approach to the body's mercuriality, sensory awareness of its existence and consciousness of its visionary and bodily manifestations. When body consciousness simply ends with awareness, then Mercury is frustrated. He wants to be freed or transformed.

In his article "The Spirit Mercurius," Jung describes how Christianity bottled up Wotan, the Germanic version of Mercury. Wotan was a wild, raving, violent, instinctive, mediumistic god whose blind animality transformed into the paradisal snake or hell's devil in Christian mythology. "Doing good" superseded being unpredictable, noisy and uncharitable. Christianity bottled Mercury.

The lumberman (the boy's father image in our fairy tale) who is working to earn a living instead of working creatively and pleasurably, also contributes to the bottling of Mercury. In the negative father's world, nothing is done just for the sake of doing it but it must have a goal in the future.

If we assume that the tree represents body sensations, then the lumberman would be someone who neglects physical experience in order to live in the ordinary world. "Killing" trees disturbs the vegetative nervous system but achieves conscious goals.

The tree-killer is an archetypal motif. Lockhart points out that when Erysichton wanted to cut down trees in Demeter's grove, he infuriated the goddess and incurred her wrath.[33] Lockhart

[32]C. G. Jung, "The Spirit Mercurius."
[33]Russell A. Lockhart, "Cancer in Myth and Dream."

quotes another fairy tale in which a king cut down trees because they angered him. They killed him in turn, while his son was inflicted with an insatiable hunger which forced him to eat himself alive.

Goals in harmony with the body gods do not ruin the vegetative nervous system. In the Bible the famous fiery bush that appeared to Moses burned without destroying its leaves. God manifested himself through the bush, through the dreambody. However, our godless lumberman is not like Moses; he decided to conquer his existential problems with ego strength alone.

We see a multi-faced criminal appearing from the bottle's amplifications. Christianity repressed instinct; science created cause-and-effect explanations and repressed mercurial unpredictability; the patriarchal work ethic denies the pleasure principle. But still there must be a factor missing in our mystery. Christianity, science and masculinity cannot be responsible for all aspects of body problems, i.e., Mercury's call for help.

If we go back to Mercury-Wotan's legend, we find a missing clue. One of the most enigmatic stories about that god is his own self-sacrifice. For nine days and nights he hung swinging from a tree "whose roots men know not," wounded by himself with his own spear. He sacrificed himself in hope of rejuvenation, for the gods, like men, are also subject to decrepitude. In vain he waited for someone to bring him food and drink. Finally, groaning with pain, he moved runes which he spied below him until their power brought him back to life.[34]

This legend has an obvious connection to our tale. We can see that our Wotan is suffering, waiting for someone to help relieve him from his bondage to a tree. Only our tale brings up a strange twist to this archetypal legend. Our Mercury seems to have forgotten who put him into his bottle—namely, himself! Mercury bottled himself, apparently in harmony with alchemical theory. Here Mercury is not only the material to be transformed; he is also the alchemist.

Mercury's self-sacrifice and drive for renewal are archetypal. In India where the body spirit is represented by the *Atman* or *purusha*, we also find the idea that the Self reincarnates in order to overcome the karma of previous lives. Mercury is the dream-

[34]*Larousse*, p. 257.

body spirit, the Atman who decides periodically to regenerate himself by entering time and space.

Thus our total real personalities, our dreambodies, apparently consciously decide to enter life and choose great difficulties which bottle them up. We decide to string ourselves up on the tree of life and to cling to a real body in order to rejuvenate ourselves. But forgetting why it chose to be reborn, the Self tries to leave its bottle by simply breaking free of worldly commitments, searching for miraculous relaxants, or even suicide.

Dear purusha, diamond body, Mercury, atman, Self—realize that *you yourself are responsible for this voluntary torture called life.* Accept the illnesses that you yourself are responsible for and realize that the meaning of your civilizing bottle is that only *it* can awaken you to your own real nature. You chose this constriction called culture in order to rejuvenate and to realize yourself. Live through your compulsions and suffer your constricting fate. See life as a disease *you* have chosen and then you will remember who you are.

According to legend, Wotan created his own knots and then loosened them.[35] At one time or another, every individual has experienced knotting—or its physiological equivalent, cramping. Knotting and cramping are central body problems created, according to legend, by the rejuvenating tendency of the Self. The human being unconsciously creates his own time pressures and cramps in order to awaken himself to his Self. This may be why we simultaneously complain about social pressures and yet continue to increase them without limit. We are sleeping biological beings who must pressure and irritate ourselves in order to awaken. Breaking out of the bottles we create for ourselves is apparently part of our physiological myth as human beings.

An example of this type of creativity comes to mind. A woman who complained about a bottled-up feeling in the chest and stomach and who had trouble catching her breath experienced an interesting process during dreambody work. She demonstrated the bottled-up feeling by surrounding and enclosing her therapist. Then she asked to switch roles and was enclosed herself. She then struggled to get out, even biting him

[35]Peter Feldman, ''Psychologische Deutung eines Odin Christus-Kreuzes aus Alemannischer Zeit.''

at one point. Again switching roles she (as the bottle) told the therapist (who was playing her) that the bottle would not let her out because she was too superficial. The bottle said that not even love for someone outside would allow the ego to go free. According to the bottle, only dance would free the woman from the enclosure. She then danced and experienced what appeared to her as utter freedom.

The night before this body work, the woman had dreamed of a superficial woman giving birth to a child who was going to die. The doctor, a mercilessly honest shaman, told the dreamer that the birth required listening to death who appeared as number 8. Her association to the number 8 was dance. In this case we see how the bottling sensation in the body—the sense of confinement, frustration and pressure—is symbolized in her dream by the merciless shaman. The bottled-up feeling is body wisdom restraining the woman from being superficial. The bottle is a sort of enforced womb in which death is being brought to birth in the dance form.

At first inspection the bottle appears to be an evil doer in the body and in our fairy tale. The bottle appears to be genetic inheritance, bacteria, overwork, religious dogma, rationalism, childhood trauma, unconsciousness, karma, public opinion or time pressure. But closer inspection of the cramping, pressuring, inhibiting aspect of problems shows that the *bottle is the dreambody's own rejuvenation requirement,* the dreambody's resistance against unconsciousness and superficiality. Freedom from this bottle occurs only at death, or at the moment when the ego is able to follow the dreambody.

We remember that the young man goes near the roots of the tree and hears a voice calling out to be set free. He pulls the bottle's cork and suddenly finds himself entangled with the murderous attack of the Spirit Mercury.

Mercury's call and resulting rage and attempt at revenge are difficult to understand without knowledge of body phenomena. Threats of murder are not infrequent phenomena in bodywork. Hiding behind apparently meaningless cramps and pain often lies the most malicious and—at first inspection—incomprehensible battle. The existential dramas reported earlier and the ultimatums in the form of ''change or else'' indicate that the spirit wanting its freedom is potentially dangerous and wily, requiring the utmost respect! The individual entering the roots of the body tree must reckon with confronting a life and death struggle whose dimensions one normally only dreams about. Confronting this spirit requires training and wisdom.

Giving Mercury his freedom may be potentially dangerous. As I have pointed out, the cramps and knots of body phenomena have important meanings. They restrict body nature in order to make it more conscious and to ensure that goals of the gods and not of the egos are fulfilled. Simply letting the spirit free could mean ignoring one's own mental and physical restrictions. None of us are free. We are all prisoners of our own processes. Dealing with these processes and meeting the conflicts arising between our natural being and the subtle requirements of individuation are a matter for active imagination.

The Role of Active Imagination

Jung's discovery of active imagination is described in great detail with many examples by Barbara Hannah in her new book, *Encounters with the Soul: Active Imagination as Developed by C. G. Jung* (Sigo Press, 1981). Active imagination is a part of dreambody work which stresses the conscious confrontation with unconscious material. This material manifests mainly through visual and auditory channels in images and voices. Dreambody work on a physical symptom, such as a stomachache, becomes active imagination when the amplification becomes an image, such as a spirit caught in a bottle. Then working with this imagery supersedes the body sensation. In fairy tales, the unconscious manifests itself in terms of imagery. The Spirit in the Bottle fairy tale allows us to experience four aspects of *active* imagination.

Finding Mercury. The first step in active imagination cannot be made by the ego alone. The unconscious (i.e., Mercury) must first manifest itself. One has to wait for "power" to appear. Only the sharp eye of the hunter picks up the empirical reality of the dreambody as it manifests itself as an unpredictable, uncontrollable power in everyday life. Mercury's first call for interaction may be a strong dream or a powerful emotion such as jealousy or paranoia, depression, inexplicable motions of the hands, other natural phenomena, body spasms and uncontrollable sensations. The unprepared person is better advised to neglect Mercury's invitation. However, the student of psychology or physiology must eventually meet the object of his or her observations and learn the methods of active imagination—call them body alchemy, meditation or creative dance.

Listening or Transforming Oneself. A person, for example, dreams of a snake. At first one may try to talk to the snake and then listen intently to see if the snake answers. Snakes are examples of unconscious phenomena which are difficult to talk to or understand.

Hence, it is frequently necessary to transform oneself so that one may converse at the level of snakes; snake to snake, so to speak. One may become a snake and talk to the original snake or actually become the original snake and then experience what its message is. The validity of an active imagination depends completely on the authenticity of the snake experience. Hence if the snake says, "What a nice day! Let's go sailing," then we know that a human being and not a snake has spoken because few snakes know about sailing.

The untrained intellect always confuses itself with figures of the unconscious. If the ego speaks to a cramped stomach and the stomach says that it is enjoying the sunshine, then this is not the stomach. It is necessary to become a cramped-up stomach in order to feel and know what the body part is thinking or saying. Only human beings speak English; one should not be surprised if a part of the unconscious does not "speak." The fact that Mercury speaks to the hero of our tale should be taken symbolically to mean that our body has experienced or discovered communication with the unconscious.

Integrating the Reactions. After having listened to Mercury, automatic reactions occur. Just as some people never hear Mercury, so many never take note of their reactions. How do you feel about what the snake did? How did it feel to be the snake? How did the stomach cramp feel? How does the rest of the body react to the stomach cramp? Does the rest of the body enjoy the stomach cramp posture? How does the entire chest area react to a heartbeat? Is there pain, panic, pleasure, excitement or what? Mercury's messages and signals polarize the psyche and create reactions that are his "partners" in communication. The most frequent partner in a discussion with dream figures is the ordinary everyday ego. The same ego may have reactions to body signals, too, but usually the strongest reactions to specific complexes in the body come from the entire physical being. Analogically speaking, the entire body is to a physical symptom as the ego is to a specific dream figure. Just as the ego tries to integrate dream experiences into itself, so the entire body integrates and becomes what is going on in a specific part of itself.

Bringing Consciousness to These Experiences. After having a beginning dialogue between Mercury and his polarization, the last step is to bring these experiences to consciousness.

Spontaneous reactions are not conscious. The most natural reaction, for example, to a body tumor that says it wants to kill is panic. This panic is due in part to the foreign quality of Mercury's announcement and is the reason why Mercury feels so omnipotent. Panic is a primary and primitive reaction, not an experience of consciousness. We must remember, however, that frequently one tries to repress the "spirits" that say they want to strangle one to death. The spirit's murderousness is not due simply to the malicious character of unconscious contents but, more than anything else, to the insensitivity to and fear of consciousness. The ego's natural reaction to an attack is of course to push it off. But psychic things cannot be pushed away. They do not disappear. They hang on and will not let go.

Our young hero must have realized this and therefore used his consciousness against Mercury instead of letting himself get polarized into a panic reaction or running from a spirit no one has ever escaped from. The young man used his consciousness and became mercurial himself. He played Mercury's game. "If you are so great, dear spirit, then please show me just what sort of magic you can do!" The boy outwitted Mercury by trying to listen to him and then by reacting with consciousness. A powerful attitude toward a dreambody content is to learn more about it. Show me yourself! Who are you? What is your nature? Why do you want to kill me? Why do you follow me? Can I use you? These questions "rebottle" the symptoms and obtain their potential gifts.

In any case, the final aspects of dreambody work and active imagination deal with the introduction of consciousness into the world of elves and demons, and the integration of unconscious signals into everyday life. Answering the following questions, for example, often enlightens the consciousness: Where am I like that snake? Where am I the stomach cramp? How am I this dream figure? When did I react or behave like that gestalt? What are my everyday problems and how does my imagination help? How is my physical behavior called into question by my body work?

Only when these questions are asked is Mercury forced to give his gifts.

The Magical Rag

The father meets the needs of reality through compulsive hard work. He cuts down trees, aspects of his own vegetative nervous system. Since his work has not been successful (he could no longer earn a living), his son has had to return from his school for lack of money. We might understand the father as the hard-working laborer behind the practice of medicine and psychotherapy.

In either case, the rag that turns metals to silver transforms the father's work tool, his axe. When the axe turns to silver, the way in which the father works is changed from "doing" to the more irrational form of work which we have named "not-doing." "Not-doing" does not mean not doing *anything,* but working in such a way that the dreambody accomplishes things without ego effort or compulsion. In not-doing the dreambody creates and the ego rests; in doing, the ego's primitive nature strikes out against work and at the same time forces itself to accomplish tasks within certain time limits. Doing implies conflict and body problems; not-doing paradoxically frees the dreambody by allowing it to obey its own laws.

Bringing the body into unison with itself in dreambody work transports one into an irrational world in which life is allowed to flow effortlessly. Body problems also frequently heal. This healing aspect is the other side of the rag. Dreambody work heals the body by relieving it from doing and by integrating symptoms as meaningful aspects of existence. After body work, Mercurial symptoms are forced to become life itself. One is not simply ill, but has become the illness so to speak. One solves a body problem by taking its point of view. Hence, the rag transforms work methods and heals the body.

I have noted that our fairy tale appeared during a period when chemistry and medicine were beginning to replace alchemical methods. It seems as if the fairy tale spoke to seventeenth and eighteenth century scientists as dreams speak to us today, saying something like

> Look here, school medicine is not all there is. You are forgetting about the body itself in your efforts to learn so-called objective methods. Remember, if you want to learn how to heal the body you must start at home, in your own forest, your own body. There, lying within your own symptoms is the spirit that makes you ill. But this very same spirit has the healing potion. If you learn about this body spirit you may be able to help the dreambody realize that it must follow its own designs. Alone, your dreambody neither heals nor destroys. Together, you and your dreambody can transform reality, alter your work methods, and relieve your symptoms.

GODFATHER DEATH

In another tale about healing we see further dreambody symbolism.

> Once there was a man who had twelve children and when the thirteenth came into the world, he could no longer find a godfather for it. So he decided to ask the first person he saw on the road. First he met God, but decided against asking him to be the godfather because God helped the rich and not the poor. When the father met the Devil, he did not ask him because he did only evil and led men astray. Finally the father accepted the third traveler, Death, because Death was fair to all. So Death attended the baptism as godfather.
>
> When the boy grew up, the godfather reappeared and took him into the forest to give him a gift. He pointed to a special herb in the forest and said, "I will make you a famous doctor. If, when you go to a sick person, I am standing at the head of the bed, give the person this herb and he will be healed. If, however, I stand at the foot of the bed, no remedy or physician in the whole world can be found to save the patient."
>
> The young man quickly became a famous doctor. But when the king fell ill, the young doctor switched the king's bed around because Death was standing at the foot. The king was healed by the doctor's trick, but Death warned his godson not to do the same again.

When the king's daughter became ill the king announced that anyone who could heal her would be king and have the girl in marriage. So when the young doctor saw Death standing at the foot of the girl's bed, he thought he could trick him once more. He switched the bed around and healed the girl.

But Death was angry and took the doctor into a cave below the earth and showed him the candles that represented the lives of the people on earth. When the doctor saw his own little flickering candle, he begged Death to put in a larger one, but Death only pretended to follow his godson's wishes and instead put out the little candle. Immediately the doctor fell dead.

The Doctor

The fairy tale doctor symbolizes prevailing medical attitudes toward the body and appears as the inner physician in dreams. This inner figure carries immense projection which can be discovered from the associations to individual dream figures. The doctor may be a great healer or a rationalist. He may be impeccable or uninterested in personal life. He is often only a chemist and falls illicitly in love with his patients. Or he is medically inadequate but humanely supreme because he listens to his patients' feelings.

Frequently the dream physician is unable to cope with the nature of the disease. In a dream of a cancer patient, a surgeon-physician—who in reality is a manly, powerful person—appeared as an insane man asking the dreamer for help. A leukemia patient dreamed that her physician said jokingly that he was a holistic doctor; but beings from another world associated to the leukemia said that they too were holistic.[36] Still another cancer patient dreamed that the last healer who could help her was called a mandala doctor. Another person, after receiving a diagnosis of cancer, dreamed that the healing medicine consisted of a spiraling rocket. In many dreams of ill persons the physician himself is responsible for the propagation of disease.

In part, the inner dream doctor symbolizes a specific dream system which is constellated as soon as the body becomes ill. He is partly the reaction of the unconscious to itself and partly a reflection of the ego's adequate or inadequate relationship to the body's mercuriality.

[36]Selma Hyman, "Death-in-Life, Life-in-Death."

Death

As the thirteenth child, our fairy tale doctor comes at the end of 12, which means at the end of a unit of time: at the end of 12 months, after midnight, at the beginning of a new unit, and hence at the edge of consciousness. The thirteenth child symbolizes the beginning of a new period characterized by phenomena beyond consciousness, beyond life. Good and evil, or God and Satan, are principles of consciousness, especially for medieval Europe. A culture that bears a thirteenth child is in the midst of a rebirth and is fascinated by death, the occult, drugs, altered states of consciousness, dreams and dying. Our present time—with its popular interest in psychology, drugs, divination and shamanism—could be characterized by the number 13.

Healers have always been connected with death. Our present tale shares many motifs with the famous story of the European healing god Asklepios. According to different legends, this god, son of Apollo or the Sun, came close to death at birth and was almost killed by fire. However, he was miraculously saved by the centaur Chiron, who, like the present godfather, tutored Asklepios and made him a healer by giving him magical herbs. (In Fig. 32 we see Asklepios worshipping Apollo who is passing overhead in a sun chariot.) Athene too is supposed to have gifted Asklepios with the healing blood of the terrible Gorgon monsters. Hades, like Death, became angry with Asklepios for stealing so many people from death and finally killed the famous healer.[37]

The story of Asklepios differs from the present tale in that Chiron, the tutor, is half-man, half-horse. In the fairy tale the healing ally is Death. The horse can symbolize the uninitiated or unenlightened body of a person who is living in the Muladhara, that is, in the unawakened ordinary world where spirits do not yet exist. Since Chiron is half-man, as a "horse-man" he symbolizes an actualized potential: advice and intelligence derived from the body's spasms, depressions and excitement. Mercury played an analogous role to the horse-man in the previous fairy tale and the body of a trained shaman is likewise a horse-man, a personal power that guides him. This is why shamans often have magical horses like Wotan's Sleipnir.

[37]Jan Schouten, *The Rod and Serpent of Asklepios.*

PHARMACOPOEA HAGANA.

D. Coster sculp.

32. Asklepios Worshipping Apollo

Death lives beneath the ground in our present tale and controls life by lighting and extinguishing candles that represent human lives. The candle-power of death appears in other forms. The image of igniting candles appears in connection with arousing body energy in yoga. Students of Siddha yoga discuss the arousal of mercuriality, kundalini, or body power in terms of candlelight. The lighting of candles is called *shaktipat,* which they explain in this way: *Shakti* is the sleeping Kundalini coiled in the base of the spine in the unawakened body. Shakti is the female goddess representing the mercuriality of the body—life energy, a spark, a strange symptom, or a special spontaneity which appears only occasionally in dreams and body spasms. The sleeping Shakti is a flickering or dormant candle waiting to be ignited.

Pat in the word Shaktipat means descent. This does not mean that a force is instilled from the outside, for the Shakti lies latent in each person's Muladhara. By his grace the guru simply awakens the dormant force and makes it active. Since grace comes from the outside, the word *pat* is used. *Gurukrip* is really a better word. *One candle is being lit from another*—this is a good analogy to understand the process.[38]

The guru is an inner or outer instructor who awakens the personality through touching the Self, a potential for life inherent in every individual. The Siddha yogis understand the arousal of the body as the igniting of one's personal candle from the burning flame of a guru. It is the power that emanates from or is projected onto an *enlightened* person that sparks the flame.

Trance is only one of the many aspects of being awakened by Shakti. Similar to our "Godfather Death" fairy tale, life is kindled whenever "death" is present. Death, Mercury, Chiron, or the "guru" can be any very real person who is in contact with his or her body, the atman or Self. Such people are neither good nor evil; in fact, they are not even necessarily related to others in a social sense. They are simply their just-so selves. They may be found in the mountains or in the city, in the form of anyone who follows his life energy and does not play social games. Depending on their temperament and education, such persons often become healers or psychologists.

[38]Swami Baba Muktananda, *The Play of Consciousness,* p. xiii. (Parentheses and italics added.)

Death appears in India as guru and instructor in the figure of Yama, the god of death and revealer of supreme knowledge. According to the Upanishads, a young Brahman who struggles to reach the underworld asks Yama to tell of man's fortune after death. Yama speaks of a "fire that leads to heaven" and of a "bridge to the supreme Brahman."[39] Death is that which is beyond consciousness. The "fire" refers to heated emotions, fevers and diseases, or powerful dreams. Yama, the timeless personality, tells the young man that the true Self or Atman can "be obtained only by the one who he [Yama] chooses" and not by self-instruction, self-education or the use of the intellect. Yama reveals that the Atman or dreambody rides in a chariot which is the real body and that this body must be trained and cultivated.[40]

Yama's first message tells the young man that enlightenment —that is, connection to the spirit—cannot be had through wishing. It occurs only through contact with death, with body symptoms. Yama himself chooses who will be enlightened; this means that not everyone can realize his true nature and become whole in this life.

According to legend, Yama is an instructor of yoga whose foremost symbol in Indian literature is a driver in his chariot.[41] The driver is the dreambody, and the chariot or horse is the real body. When Yama tells the student that the Atman rides in a chariot which is the real body and which must be trained, he is giving the basic instruction of yoga: make the horse and chariot conscious through becoming aware of physiological or dream-body signals. Awareness is inspired not only by Yama, of course, but by disease and fear of death. The purpose implicit in Yama's instruction is to differentiate the chariot from the driver, the body from the soul. Yama as dreambody energy paradoxically teaches about body; the dreambody teaches about itself—or yoga teaches yoga, according to an ancient Indian text.[42]

Thus if we patiently study dreams, in time they themselves produce tutelary figures who instruct about the nature of life

[39]Eliade, *Yoga: Immortality and Freedom,* p. 118.
[40]Ibid., p. 272.
[41]Ibid.
[42]Ibid., p. 39. "Yoga must be known by means of Yoga; Yoga manifests itself through Yoga. . . ."

and even about dream work itself. Likewise, by patiently studying and amplifying body signals, one meets an inner-body guru,
or energy, which gives instruction about how to move the
body. This enlightenment, symbolized in our fairy tale by the
candles of Death, also produces energies which stimulate
various body centers with "fire or warmth,"[43] even causing
the person to assume yoga postures. These centers and postures
are archetypal potentials which spontaneously create themselves in meditation and body work when the body is allowed
to move in its own rhythm and form.

The body teaches about itself as soon as the individual begins
to train it. The body's limitations, mortality, and closeness to
death can be discovered, as well as the body's intelligence and
the dreambody. Dreambody consciousness appears in yoga as
the final goal which the body itself strives for. In India, experiencing the subtle body is achieving ultimate freedom; consciousness of this body makes the yogi a "dead man in life,"[44]
experiencing the freedom of death by differentiating the real
personality from the body and worldly affairs. Becoming a dead
man in life means integrating death, being free to dream and
loving this dream.

We also find Death as a guru in the teachings of Castaneda's
don Juan, who says, "Death is the only wise advisor that we
have. Whenever you feel, as you always do, that everything is
going wrong and you're about to be annihilated, turn to your
death and ask if it is so. Your death will tell you that you're
wrong; that nothing really matters outside its touch. Your death
will tell you, 'I haven't touched you yet.'"[45] The figure of death
assumes many configurations in don Juan's teachings. He is the
"ally," "agreements" from the environment; he is the wisdom
inherent in the body and the spirit of the nocturnal desert.

Although death rarely appears as a specific gestalt in dreams,
death fantasies prevail in people of all ages. In my experience
most of these fantasies try to create radical changes in life at a
time when the ego feels blocked against the apparently inflexible forces of the world. Many death fantasies want immediate
change whether or not an actual illness is present.

[43]Lu K'uan Yü, *Taoist Yoga*, p. xviii.
[44]Eliade, *Yoga: Immortality and Freedom*, p. 272.
[45]Carlos Castaneda, *Journey to Ixtlan*, p. 55.

In Moody's collection of experiences, "death appears as a luminous gaseous being of light" which communicates with the ego when it is out of the body.[46] Death is also an enlightener and tests the dying, typically insisting that love problems be worked out and that education continue.[47]

One of my dying friends told me that being dead is a most confusing experience because "when you want to tie your shoes, the laces disintegrate into atoms." Or, he said, you go downtown but suddenly find your real body on the floor of a room in your house. Such dying experiences[48] indicate that dying itself manifests the dreambody. Dreambody experiences near death are like living dreams; one comes and goes, sees and experiences, but apparently simply cannot communicate to others through sound, light or touch.

According to our fairy tale, Death lives beneath the ground with magical candles. But Death can also appear above the ground in the form of a figure at the foot or head of the bed. His appearance above the ground refers to dreambody manifestations such as dreams, body motions, illnesses, strong visions and fantasies.

Dreams occur in reduced states of consciousness and ego awareness, but meditation reveals the exact nature of these states to the wakeful ego. Our tale talks about these states in terms of lighting and extinguishing candles. Instead of describing how these states appear, I recommend an experiment: When you become tired during the accomplishment of some task—such as reading this book or conversing with someone— stop what you are doing, close your eyes, and focus on your breathing or heartbeat. Meditate upon tiredness. Eventually, ignition occurs. Either the old activity is turned on again with a different emphasis, or another new activity appears in consciousness. The change in the old and the creation of a new focus is an experience of Death's candlelighting below the ground. Discovering and experiencing the kindling of new energy gives one a personal experience of Death as an ally, teacher, and dreambody.

[46]Raymond Moody, *Life After Life.*
[47]Ibid.
[48]Garfield Charles, "Ego Functioning, Fear of Death and Altered States of Consciousness."

The Ill Person

The figure of an ill person appears frequently in dreams, just as illness is a main concern of consciousness. Such dreams are especially important in understanding the body. The first step in working with such dreams is to find out who the ill figure is. What does this ill person do for a living? What is the psychological behavior of this person? What is the nature of the disease? Is it curable or fatal? What has he or she been doing? The next step is to associate to the disease itself. Where is one sick? What part of the real body is ill? In my experience *every ill dream figure symbolizes a physiological disturbance as well as a psychological complex.*

The associations to the ill dream figure tell the analyst how to treat the dream figure, the real body, and the life problem of the dreamer. For example, a man who dreamed that his girl friend was dying of throat cancer associated to his girl that she was terrified to speak in public. He associated to her sickness that he himself had a chronically sore throat. Her terminal dream illness meant that Death was standing at the foot of her bed and no treatment would help. In other words, the difficulty in speaking and the sore throat could no longer be worked on; the unconscious simply wanted the man to get up and speak, to stop thinking about how to do it, and to suffer the consequences. The unconscious was advising him against further analysis of the speaking problem and against further efforts to cure his chronically sore throat. Now Death itself wanted to rule. This man had to stop making preparations, let chance rule, and follow his body.

Death stands at the head of the bed if illness or ill dream figures do not have fatal associations. For example many people dream that they have the flu. In reality they often only feel tired. Since the flu is normally not fatal, Death is, symbolically speaking, standing at the head of the bed. The unconscious is saying that the head needs to change. Such people do not have to stop everything they are doing but must change their attitudes toward life.

Many ancient healers used their patients' dreams to see where the healing spirit stood. Greek physicians, for example, thought healing occurred through the advent of Asklepios in dreams.

Likewise, Serapis, an Egyptian healing god, also appeared in dreams. Early European medicine also used divination. Asklepian priests favored large white crystals which indicated whether healing would come or not.[49] According to Eric Maple, "a crystal or special stone was placed in a divining cup filled with water. If on its removal from the cup the stone was found to be dull and lustreless, the patient's health prospects were considered grave. However, if the stone glistened, there were good expectations of recovery."[50] Besides dreams and stones, mirrors were also used. In captromancy the patient suspended a small mirror attached to a thread into a fountain before the temple of Ceres, the Earth Goddess.[51] If the mirror showed a distorted view, death was to come. If the face was happy, health would soon appear. The scrying stone, which emitted a thin whistling noise, was also used in such divination.[52]

Hence divination was used by ancient physicians to decide where Death was standing. If I have any doubts about whether to begin work with an analysand, I ask the *I Ching* where death stands relative to the work. I do not interpret the answer as a final statement about the analysand's fate but rather understand the *I Ching* as an advisor, telling me whether or not *I* am able to work with that person.

Gods of divination, the earth goddesses, and healing gods may also appear in the form of intuition or body reactions. Intuition is often a product of wishes, fears, complexes, but occasionally, spontaneous fantasies which arise during transactions with someone are signs from "Death" about whether the work should be continued or a specific subject dropped.

One of the therapist's most frequent body experiences is the feeling of exhaustion. Exhaustion and fatigue are symptoms that the spark, the fire, the candle, the kundalini is no longer in the work and that a candle is flickering. The therapist's energy often flickers when the "patient" is not focusing on central problems and experiences. If the "doctor" follows the patient's conscious interests instead of staying where the energy is, he continues to listen when his interest is elsewhere. In this

[49]Eric Maple, *The Ancient Art of Occult Healing,* p. 11.
[50]Ibid., p. 12.
[51]Ibid.
[52]Ibid.

moment the doctor's Death tells him through tiredness that a change in mind, a change in focus, is necessary. The medicine for his lack of energy and for the problem being worked on is to change the subject and to wait and see what new subject Death wants to light up. Just as our doctor has trouble following his Death in the fairy tale, so the modern person may have trouble following the direction of his energy because of collective rules and fears of not being liked.

If an analysis tends to be exhausting over a long period of time, Death is often standing at the foot of the therapeutic work. The "doctor" should admit that he knows nothing that can help the person and that the situation should be left to fate. This admission sometimes revives both the doctor and the patient. Strange as it may seem, however, many ill people do not really want help. They even become angry when the best help arrives. They frequently need ordinary relationships, not therapy, or they may have to do their own work, using the "doctor" as collaborator. When inner complexes persuade people that they cannot help themselves or that their "illnesses" are incurable, any form of "help" actually *hinders* development. Such situations should be left up to Death—that is, to a spontaneous spark in the dreamer's psyche and body.

Death and Healing

Just as our fairy-tale father could not ask God or the Devil (either goodness or evil) to be the godfather-principle for his son (the father's new development in consciousness), so many ill persons need to contact their Death in order to reorient themselves to life. Death is neither good nor evil but rather the nature of body energy. People must take the risk of sacrificing their conscious and cultural principles and follow the unpredictable dictates of the body.

In many terminal cases, death itself must *literally* rule. Psychologizing about physiology, searching for the right medicine, using the best doctor, or finding magical healers only seem to aggravate nature. The less one tries to do anything to hold back Death in such situations the better the "sick" people feel. Their dream messages say that fate itself must rule even though this means giving up personal history and even life itself at an early age. The only peace such persons find in the midst of their turmoil appears when they finally let go and follow the Tao, the eternal flow of things.[53]

In such cases one always wonders whether Death could have been put off had the flow been followed earlier. No one knows. Dreams often say no. Without having resisted the Tao, its value could never have been discovered. Dreams of ill persons are often paradoxical. I remember one person whose dreams first portrayed Death as the enemy from the other side who had to be fought at all cost; later dreams showed Death as a friendly endless river which asked to be loved. Death gives a plant as a medicine for disease in our tale—hence Death gives death for life. What is the meaning of this paradox?

Death's medicine for those who can be healed is a special herb from the forest (similar to the plant Asklepios received from Chiron or a serpent). Plants have been used by healers since earliest times and are still applied today by shamans to cure the ill. For example the yegé vine induces altered states of consciousness and is used by South American shamans to produce visions and dreams of healing serpents. When the dreamer develops a positive relation to the dream serpents, the disease is healed. Such hallucinatory drugs have been used widely in Europe by witches and healers since earliest times.[54]

The plants in our tale are vegetative nourishment. "Vegetative" implies involuntary action and life in the body. Involuntary activities include the peristaltic motions of the viscera and heart, pupil dilation and general states induced by meditation, dreams and drugs.

Vegetative types of experiences are closely related to death. Meditation, for example, which brings the yogi back to the womb and which allows him to become a plant, aims at making

[53]Working with people who are dying has increased my respect for Death and the processes it creates in the body. They have encouraged me to let Death speak directly. Since Death is subtle body energy, I experimented with Death's flow at first by encouraging the ill person to remain motionless until some sort of fantasy or body motion occurred spontaneously. Then we amplified those motions by slightly increasing their intensity, watching them transform into other motions. When these non-ego movements of the body were amplified, spontaneous insight occurred, religious experiences happened, and in practically every case the ill person felt better physically. I took these results as a possible indication of how to integrate Death into analytical work or dreambody work. I discuss this topic in greater detail in Chapter 5.

[54]Michael J. Harner, ed., *Hallucinogens and Shamanism.*

the yogi a "dead man in life." Dreams too bring one to the
other world, and drug trips frequently travel to a border of the
beyond. For the yogi the plant world symbolizes death and
prebirth experiences because in meditation he becomes a plant
and realizes earlier lives.

Although the first response to the appearance of illness is normally a mixture of fear and irritation, the individual interested
in physiological impulses can use them to increase awareness of
the vegetative nature of the body. Studying the ailing heart, for
example, can reveal the vegetative nervous system and the
thread upon which life itself hangs. Meditation on a chronic
pain may unveil Death as a cancer image which emits existential
messages such as "Change now." Ingesting such vegetative
nourishment given by "Death" reveals the source of life.
Respecting this source connects consciousness to subtle energy
and also to "psychological" complexes. When Death stands at
the head of the bed in disease states, its healing plant is the
vegetative experience of disease itself and its implication about
how to live. Disease can be a teacher about life! Death brings
disease, but teaches about vegetative experience, the origin of
life.

The idea that Death creates but also heals disease is the basis
of homeopathy. Our tale says: the cure for death is death. According to homeopathy, increasing symptoms heal. The theory
of homeopathy is that small dosages of given poisons which are
known to produce symptoms like the ones of a given disease
produce cures by unknown mechanisms.

> The fundamental generalization, the bedrock of homeopathy,
> is that the most successful drug for any given occasion will be
> the drug whose own symptomatology presents the clearest and
> closest resemblance to the symptom-complex of the sick person
> in question. Briefly, "Likes should be treated with likes," the
> "simillium," the most-resembling drug, should be preferred.
> Whenever this rule is followed (even unconsciously) homeo-
> pathy is practiced.[55]

The idea that the unconscious heals itself is found elsewhere.
For example, in the Mercury tale the spirit that was capable of
murder also gave the healing potion. This corresponds with the

[55]Charles Wheeler, *An Introduction to the Principles and Practice of
Homeopathy*, p. 3.

alchemical idea that the prima materia contains its own healing. In stories that follow, an apparently murderous water god gives water as a healing potion and a killer snake is healed by another which also heals human beings.

The homeopathic idea that "poison" cures itself is also found in psychology. Carl Rogers discovered that simply repeating what someone said increases consciousness immensely. The Rogerian idea can also be applied to dream work. If an interpreter repeats a given dream over and over again to the dreamer, the latter often spontaneously understands aspects of the dream message. The gestalt therapist amplifies dreams by asking the dreamer to actually become a dream figure. Jung amplified dreams by using personal associations, increasing the meaning of the personal with mythological and scientific information, and also by using imagination.

In the Mercury fairy tale, the psychological process of amplifying unconscious contents until they produce their own solution is symbolized by the alchemist's bottle. One puts the process back in the bottle, cooks and stews it until it produces the panacea. Put Mercury back into the bottle, think about him consciously, and then he himself gives the magical rag. Alchemy amplifies or cooks a process until it transforms of its own accord.

This concept of amplification is also found in the modern idea of biofeedback. In this science a body signal is amplified by increasing awareness of it with the use of an instrument which feeds back information to the observer. This feedback stimulates reaction and control over the signal. Biologists do not yet know the exact connection between the feedback signal and its final control because a causal or electrochemical circuit between the signal and its manipulation cannot be found.[56] We only know that the body finds its own ways of controlling signals once they are made conscious through amplification. The homeopathic effect, in my opinion, is based on the same feedback-amplification process.

Yoga too works with internal feedback, although the yogi is not likely to formulate his experiences in these terms. Yogis discovered long ago that one cannot repress fantasies, pains and pleasures that appear during meditation. So the yogi tolerates or

[56]Leo DiCara, ed., *Limbic and Automatic Nervous System Research.*

even amplifies the disturbing signals. In this way they disappear. Opening up to "what is" is called "Zen" or "beginner's mind" by the Zen Buddhist meditators.[57] What seems to happen in most "toleration" meditation is that one subliminally works out the meaning of a disturbing fantasy and makes internal changes without their becoming conscious to the intellect.

Another historical aspect of amplification is found in the so-called "doctrine of signatures." Vogel describes this doctrine and its relationship to American Indian medicine as follows:

> The doctrine of signatures played an important role in Indian medicine, as it once did in European medicine. "Like cures like" was the essence of this belief; thus, yellow plants were good for jaundice; red ones were good for the blood. Some part of the plant might resemble the organ of the body it was designed to cure, according to this belief. Reminders of the former prevalence of such conceptions among Europeans are indicated by plant names such as hepatica, formerly believed to be useful in liver complaints, and lungwort, once believed valuable in pulmonary infections.[58]

The Indians used dogbane (*Apocynum cannabinum*) for worms and snake root (*Aristolochia serpentaria*) for fits or contortions because of the appearance of these plants. Elm bark was used for bleeding lungs because of its slippery quality, and bloodroot was used to prevent bleeding because of the red juice contained in it.[59]

The Indians also amplified dreams in order to heal:

> In a report from the Onondaga country in 1676, we are told that the medicine men persuaded the parents of a sick girl that she had seen nine feasts in dreams, and that if they gave these feasts she would be cured. Thus followed days of revelry, which seemed diabolical to the fathers.[60]

The use of amplification in modern body work is less known to us. Dreambody work is based on perceiving a physiological signal and allowing it to amplify itself or encouraging it to do so through the use of various techniques discussed in Chapter 6. Frequently such work produces its own solution. Amplifying

[57]Shunryu Suzuki, *Zen Mind, Beginner's Mind.*
[58]Virgel Vogel, *American Indian Medicine*, p. 30.
[59]Ibid.
[60]Ibid., pp. 18, 19.

internal pains and pleasures often leads to a sort of "satori" which requires no further intellectual work.

For example, a person suffering from diarrhea consulted me recently. The homeopathic plant for this disease was the disease itself. The disturbed body area amplified itself and was suddenly imagined to say, "I am the stomach and intestines and I refuse to accept any more food. Fate has moved into me and will not allow me to digest anything and gives me pain when I decide to live as I have always lived. All I need is a long rest with nothing to do." At this point the person was "enlightened," complained about all there was to do and realized that the effort to "do" had to be dropped.

New orienting concepts which can be used in dreambody work appear in fairy tales. Final goals such as awareness of the dreambody appear in the Mercury fairy tale. "Godfather Death" has now provided the concept of amplification as a further principle in dreambody work.

The King and the Princess

The drama in our tale occurs when the king falls ill. The doctor switches the king's bed around so that Death stands at the head and the king is healed. When the princess gets sick, the doctor does the same, but Death becomes furious and kills the doctor for his disobedience.

Von Franz has amplified these figures in her extensive research on fairy tales.[61] The king symbolizes the principles of consciousness. For example, some of the guiding principles of modern consciousness are to help others, to support the poor, to be social and so on. The daughter of the king symbolizes the feelings associated with these principles, the eros or feeling pattern that results from given principles.

Who would the king and the princess be for the doctor? To begin with, the king represents the consciousness and collective values of the doctor's patients. If Death stands at the foot of the king's bed and the doctor saves the king, then the doctor supports his patient's sick conscious values that are trying to die. Whether or not the "doctor" supports the revolutionary tendencies in his patients or supports only the introverted side of these tendencies is an individual matter, revealed by a pa-

[61]Marie-Louise von Franz, *Introduction to the Psychology of Fairy Tales.*

tient's dreams. If the doctor neglects the drive to actually change the collective, then he does his patient a potential misdeed and also endangers himself, because Death wants the king to die. Sometimes the world must really be changed.

The princess becomes sick and must also die. If the doctor tries to save the princess, then he helps his patients to adapt to the sick-feeling standards of culture instead of encouraging them to develop a new code of feeling ethics based upon death, that is, the spontaneity of a given momentary situation. If the princess dies, then Death rules feelings and one simply has to follow the moment.

Our present culture has an ailing princess. People are nice to one another in a very unreal way. Aggression, sexuality and negativity are either utterly repressed or else unethically unleashed. The result of such false and chaotic feelings is that the real messages people want to communicate become "stuck" in the body in the form of nervousness or untamed affect.

The doctor's inner king symbolizes his collective professional principles. If the king is ill, then the principles of his profession are sick. For example, the concept of "therapy" is a common principle, a "king" for the modern doctor. According to this principle, people who are ill must be healed. And indeed, most doctors heal regardless of where Death may be standing.

In our tale Death allows the king to live after he is saved but kills the doctor when he saves the daughter against Death's orders. The king may live—that is, the doctor's professional identity as a healer may continue—but the princess must die. He has to drop his feelings about the importance of healing. The princess symbolizes the feeling of self-importance and the acts of nursing and loving people in order to heal them. The reason Death calls these feelings and acts into question is that the unconscious is not necessarily loving toward the sick attitudes of ailing people. If the doctor nurses the sick attitudes of his patients instead of telling them to change, then the doctor becomes identified with the patient. Then *both* have unreal and false feelings.

The present fairy tale speaks about collective processes, about the death of the king and princess of medicine. It may be shocking to present-day healers to hear that the principles behind their often undebated behavior must die or change. The collective is interested in healing and holds the healing principle high above everything else.

Within the field of psychology alone new treatments and tricks are developing almost as fast as the number of diseases themselves. Modern medicine is becoming increasingly important and is being aided by the uncritical application of ancient techniques such as yoga, acupuncture and shamanistic healing.

But there is something wrong in the uncritical tendency to heal. It neglects the messages of Death and tries at all costs to dull the intensity of body signals in order to reduce suffering. Death is not listened to but marched over in an effort to overcome time itself. The healing attitude has contributed to the population explosion. But the most immediate result of the ailing healing attitude is that it suffocates potential consciousness and development. Many body messages expound violent existential warnings about the necessity for instantaneous change. If these messages are consistently blurred with pain killers, relaxants and surgery, psychological death results. Then human beings are turned into robots directed by the frail so-called scientific consciousness of others.

The collective significance of Godfather Death seems to me to indicate that if medicine is not critical of its healing goals then therapy will fail. How? Will Death create diseases that cannot be healed? Do certain diseases now exist as a result of our healing tendency? Would these apparently intractable diseases disappear if we stopped trying to resist them?

According to our tale Death appears as the self-governing body energy that first emerges in the form of symptoms and diseases. But illness is only the superficial manifestation of body energy. Beneath the surface of the earth *the spirit of disease appears as the spirit and meaning behind life*. This spirit creates energy for given tasks.

When the energy for these tasks disappears, Death is calling the methods and meaning of the tasks into question. Either a change in attitude and a transformation of compulsive "doing" is required, or the task should be left up to fate and the body. In the former case, amplifying body symptoms will create the necessary change in attitude and simultaneously reduce compulsion. In the latter case, if energy for the task is consistently missing, then the work must be dropped. If one continues in spite of all indications, consciousness will be obliterated as the dreambody extinguishes personal life.

THE GODFATHER'S SECRETS OF LIFE

The mercurial spirit, the dreambody, is amplified by the following fairy tale, which ends better than the previous one. Grimm's "Godfather"[62] goes approximately as follows:

Once upon a time there was a man who had so many children that he had to ask all the people in the world to be godfathers. To find a godfather for his new son, he consulted his dreams.

He dreamed that he asked the first person he met, so when he awoke he asked the first person outside his gate to be godfather. This man gave him a glass of "wonderful water" which could heal as long as the godfather stood at the head of the patient. If he stood at the foot, then all was in vain.

So the man became a famous healer and even cured the king and the king's child twice. But the third time the godfather was standing at the foot of the child's bed, and so the child had to die.

The doctor wanted to know more about the godfather and visited his home. On the first floor he met a broom and shovel arguing with one another. They said the godfather was on the second floor, but the doctor only found dead fingers there which told him the godfather was on the third floor. There he met skulls which told him to look on the fourth floor. But there the doctor found fish cooking themselves; they said to look on the fifth floor.

When at last the doctor reached the godfather's room, he looked through the keyhole and saw horns on his godfather's head. As he entered the room, the godfather quickly pulled a sheet over himself. When the doctor asked about the things he had seen on the four floors below, the godfather became irritated and said that the broom and shovel were the maid and butler talking; the fingers on the second floor were roots of the scorzonera plant; the skulls on the third floor were cabbages and so on. The godfather became so furious that the doctor ran away. Our tale ends with the question: What would have happened to the doctor is he had not escaped when he did?

[62]*Grimm's Fairy Tales,* no. 42.

The godfather in this story shares similar features with "God-father Death." However, his medicine is water and his home is not a cave but a house filled with parapsychological things. This tale amplifies the nature of the spirit of life.

Water

In the beginning of the tale the doctor dreams that he should ask the first person he meets to be godfather. Dreaming of asking the first person to be godfather means that one should ask the next moment in time to be one's protector or father. The Chinese would say, "Let the Tao be your guide." The main symbols for the Tao are streaming, change, horned dragons and the flow of water (Fig. 33). *Aqua vitae,* or water of life, was associated with Mercury, the sap of life and "sparkling water,"[63] The astrological symbol of the water bearer, Aquarius, is pictured pouring water onto the ground, portraying how winter rains nourish potential life in the springtime.

Dreams of water often refer to rebirth experiences. I am reminded of the rains mentioned in the poetry of a woman suffering from schizophrenia who went through her "insanity" under the controlled environment of the Laing Clinic in England and who was reborn through her ecstasy and suffering.[64] She wrote of rains bringing new life out of an old dead tree. Here, water was the violence and healing quality of her experiences.

Water appeared in a healing scene I recently observed. A modern healer laid her hands on a patient saying:

Imagine the light, release all emotions, see the golden beam of light. This is god. Breathe the light into your heart center. This is the perfect heart of understanding. Feel love in your heart for yourself, feel the heart center, experience the heart, this light is perfect harmony, when it is present there no other element can live in you, it is energy, cleaning out your aura, it is water, crystal clear water which overflows and circulates in the body, it is perfect light. No one is in your aura, energy and love are there, you can use this same feeling or light to clean out other things in yourself, use this for cleansing . . .[65]

---

[63]*CW,* Vol. 13, pp. 237ff.
[64]R. Boyers and Robert Ortill, eds., *R. D. Laing and Anti-Psychiatry,* pp. 238ff.
[65]Michael Harner, ed., *Hallucinogens and Shamanism,* pp. 15ff.

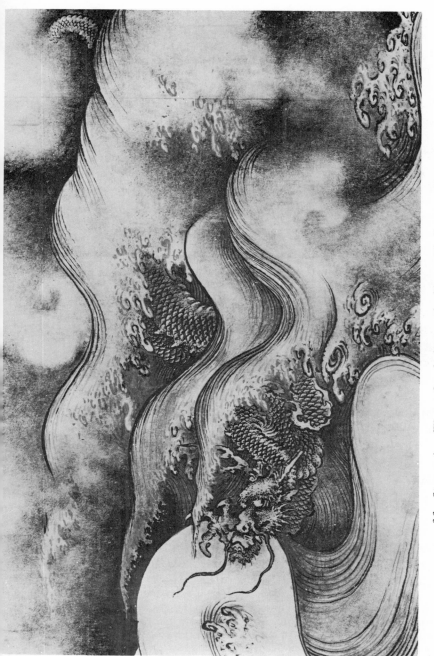

33. *Streaming Water Symbolizing the Tao with Dragon Powers in the Vortices*

The references to light and water connect Godfather Death's candles from the previous tale to the water of the present healing god. In healing ceremonies, light, water, love, release of emotions, energy flow, circulation, harmony and crystal clear water are all descriptions of curative experiences. The water is a description of free flowing energy which cleans the body by unlocking egotism and its resulting cramps.

Vegetation is closely connected to water in many myths. For example, the ancient Slavic peoples employed water and water plants in getting rid of demons. The tear weed was used with the following prayer:

> Tear weed, tear weed, thou has wept much and for a long time, but thou has gained little. May thy tears not flow in the open field, and thy sobs not sound over the blue sky. Frighten wicked demons, demi-demons and old witches. If they do not submit to thee then drown them in thy tears.[66]

The explicit nature of the demons is not explained, but I have found that the worst demons are insensitive attitudes toward the body. When people finally feel their body center, they experience extreme loneliness and sadness because the body center, the Self, has been neglected in the rush and pressure of everyday life. As soon as they reach this center they often break down, wracked with sobs, crying out their sadness. At least temporarily this may dissolve the divisive rigidity characteristic of consciousness.

The harmonizing and unifying aspect of water is found and worshipped by the Slavs in their god, Kupala (which means bathe). According to folk tales, "dead water" allows severed members of heroes to come together and "live water" resuscitates them. Also, to cure sickness, one goes to a spring and begs the water's pardon, throwing a piece of bread into it, repeating the ancient exorcism, "I come to thee, little water-mother, with head bowed and repentant. Forgive me, pardon me . . . and ye, too, ancestors and forefathers of the water."[67]

---

[66]*Larousse*, p. 296. We can compare these healing statements with those of a South American shaman entering a trance: "He had drunk . . . faint lines and forms began to appear . . . and shrill music . . . the spirit helpers arose around him. The power of the drink fed them . . . the sound of rushing water filled his ears, and listening to its roar, he knew he possessed the power of . . . the first shaman. Now he could see. . . ."
[67]Ibid.

The plant-vegetation-water symbolism is basic to dreambody understanding. The sap of plants flows in the body of the enlightened yogi.[68] In India lack of flow in the imaginary veins and arteries which carry energy and blood is blamed for illness. Cleaning these conduits and reestablishing flow is all-important. The purpose of yoga is to free "the posture from any blockages or kinks which may be inhibiting it . . . there is a resistance at some point to the flow of energies. In fact, all disease is merely a restriction of the flow of life force in a particular area. . . . nadis have to be cleared of blockages (through yoga and meditation) and enlarged. Exercises and postures which involve bending, twisting and stretching the spine fall into this category of generally promoting greater energy flow throughout the system."[69]

The Indian subtle body picture has a specific place for the experience of fluidity—the sacrum of the spine. Here, body energy expresses itself in terms of watery motions (see picture of water chakra, Fig. 17, Chapter 2). Ripeness, sexuality, urine, semen, aridity, dryness, smoothness and taste are some of the qualities of this area.[70] Lack of fluidity is held responsible for arthritis, impotence and dry skin.

Healing wells in Europe related to "pagan water spirits" and the "old gods" had the power to cure sickly children, renew strength, heal ulcers and arthritis.[71] The religious reformation of the sixteenth century did not succeed in uprooting the water cult, and even today many people in Wales still visit healing wells in their land.

Healing waters, and hence the water healer in our fairy tale, defy scientific and Christian tradition because healing cannot be controlled or mechanistically explained. The healing gods Mercury, Death, Yama and the water spirits symbolize the unknown, in contrast to Christ who is king of the light. The flow gods, the Tao, continuity and boundarylessness symbolize direct experiences of the unconscious which cannot be predicted or controlled by the conscious mind.

Since the water is a healing agent, the diseases it cures must be characterized by rigidity. But rigidity has many aspects.

[68]Eliade, *Yoga: Immortality and Freedom,* p. 66.
[69]Peter Rendel, *Introduction to the Chakras,* p. 48.
[70]Ibid.
[71]Eric Maple, *The Ancient Art of Occult Healing,* pp. 20, 21.

Whenever a complex exists, consciousness rigidifies and tries to steer around the strong emotions connected with the core of the complex. Water therapy allows the complexes to speak, encourages the body to dance its own rhythm and lets the unpredictable come alive. A water experience is holistic and unifies the entire personality so that ego, Self, dreams, body, inner and outer come together in one human being.

The more rigid the ego and the more powerful a governing complex, the more threatening the flow of the body or the psyche appears. A rigid and frightened personality becomes terrified, split off from nature, and cannot believe that a Self or a body consciousness exists that can organize behavior once ego rulership is given up.

For example, a woman who was educated in a very strict religious sect and who had backaches and allergies told me that her main body experience was cold hands. Her hands wanted warmth from someone, but as soon as she touched another person, she could not face him. "It is not good to have needs, or to be weak," she said. "It is important to be strong and to give and not have to take!" At that point she stopped her flow process. Later when she dreamed of being imprisoned by religious sectarians she could see her situation clearly.

How does the flow god react to such a block? The night after her cold-hand experience she dreamed that the whole world was flooded; she alone could enter an ark and be rescued. The water god was "standing at the foot," so to speak, of her religious sectarians who like the early Jews no longer had a relationship to God. A flood covered the earth, leaving only the dreamer. She wanted to change, but her complexes inhibited her from living and aggravated her psychosomatic ailments.

The examples of water processes in psychotherapy, the appearance of water as a symbol of healing, physical mobility and emotional fluidity in mythology and the concept of water as an example of Taoistic insight in healing ceremonies show that water stands for fluid expressiveness. Water is medicine against the rigidification of intuition, physical mobility and feeling. When the godfather gives a glass of water to his son, he is giving back the spontaneous life flow to ill people.

Because of his relationship to flow processes our doctor became famous and healed the king's family. (The symbolism of king and princess was discussed earlier in this chapter.) However, unlike the doctor in the preceding tale, our present physician followed his "godfather" to the best of his ability. He did not turn the beds around in order to fulfill his egotistical desires. Instead, he followed the patterns of fate without asking about their meaning or implications.

The Broom and Shovel

When the doctor visits the godfather's house he sees a strange assortment of parapsychological events. To understand them we may associate godfather's horns to the devil, and recall that the godfather's relatives in the other fairy tales are Death and Mercury. In other words, godfather is another symbol of the dreambody which is responsible for all spontaneous manifestations in the body and in the dream world.

The godfather's house has five stories, and he himself lives on the fifth. Five is an archetypal body number; there are five extremities to our body: five fingers and toes on each hand and foot, five senses, etc. Each floor of the five-story house therefore represents a particular aspect of the body god's totality. To understand the spirit in the body we need to investigate aspects of the body not seen in the previous two tales.

Remember that on the first floor the doctor finds a broom and shovel arguing with one another. In the period out of which this fairy tale grew, the broom was the instrument associated with feminine tasks. The broom keeps the house in order; it symbolizes home and family coherence, eros and feeling, which tie people together. The shovel is more closely related to archetypal, masculine tasks. It is used to dig, to uncover, to discover, to change and transform. The shovel symbolizes work methods; the broom the cultural principles of feeling.

In our tale the broom and shovel behave as if they had a consciousness of their own. In terms of shamanism, the tools symbolize not-doing. The not-doing function of eros would be the appearance of the unconscious in feelings and relationship—in other words, spontaneous unpredictable expressiveness. The not-doing of the shovel would be a manifestation of the unconscious in ordinary work. For a magical healer, not-doing means letting his hands operate on the body in the way *they* choose. Since the doctor uses not-doing in his practice, he is not particularly surprised when he sees the broom and shovel acting autonomously or parapsychologically in the godfather's house. The doctor does not "do" things. His body processes accomplish his tasks effortlessly.

But our doctor has the typical problems of many healers who relate to their flow processes only in their work. Their brooms and shovels do magical things, but they are not enough in touch with their inner processes to know that every event has a specific meaning for their own personal lives. Not-doing is a function of the Self, of one's personal myth. Parapsychological events are aspects of one's own inner drama and fit together only when this drama is known.[72] Otherwise, individual magical events seem to conflict or argue with one another.

The Fingers

On the next floor, the healer meets fingers that can talk. These fingers have archetypal relatives in ancient Greece. On Mount Ida, the Earth Goddess Rhea was about to give birth to Zeus when she put her hands into the soil to support herself. Suddenly the mountain brought forth as many spirits as there were fingers. These spirits assisted at birth and were called Dactyls, or Fingers.[73] There were 20 right-hand fingers, and 32 left-hand spirits. The right were smiths, the left magicians. These fingers were connected in Greek mythology with healers, smiths, magicians, craftsmen and, of course, dwarfs. Greek mythology is specific. The right-handed fingers can break the magic and spells created by the left ones.

Fingers act autonomously. Fritz Perls should be credited as the modern discoverer of the Dactyls, since he encourages autonomously moving hands and fingers to gestalt themselves and to talk.[74] While I was talking with a patient, his right-hand index finger continuously went to his head and scratched his scalp. Instead of asking him what he was doing, I told him to let his hand continue what it was doing and to let his finger speak.

[72]In his article on "Synchronicity" (*CW,* Vol. 8), Jung mentions many parapsychological or synchronicitic events which are organized by the meaning factor in personal life.
[73]Carl Kerényi, *The Gods of the Greeks,* pp. 83–86.
[74]Federick Perls, *Gestalt Therapy Verbatim.*

To make the story short, the finger said it was not really scratching the scalp but trying to massage it, because it was tense. It did not let blood run up through into the hairs and would not let thoughts through. In other words, this person was "narrow"-minded in the sense that he did not let his thoughts flow.

The fingers are manifestations of helpers of the Great Earth Mother, the unconscious. The unconscious was trying to say something, trying to bring something to consciousness, to birth, and the fingers were really helping. I could not have brought out the narrow-mindedness for my patient as well as his fingers did. They were the healers and smiths, workers of the godfather.

Godfather interprets the fingers as the roots of the scorzonera plant (scorzonera is from an old French word for serpent). The fingers are thus the roots of the serpentine function, that is, of the autonomic nervous system. Since the scorzonera plant is edible, we may assume that the godfather wants his healer to "eat" his healing fingers, that is, to digest them as if they were roots of information. Only if the ego *looks* at the fingers do they appear as autonomous functions. If they *speak,* they appear as midwives of the unconscious.

The Skulls

The magical fingers are only the second manifestation of godfather. They point to another level, the skulls. In ancient Europe, skulls were said to contain the genie or life spirit of the deceased.[75] The head was oracular. Even a sneeze was a prophetic agreement with what one was saying or thinking.[76] We find talking skulls in fairy tales and in shamanic episodes in which skulls act as oracles. Eliade talks about shamanic initiations in which the shaman-to-be must visualize his dismembered body and his skull.[77] The English language contains expressions indicating that a spirit is located in the head: A person without any spirit is called a deadhead.

The skulls symbolize the intuitive function of the healer, his mediumistic ability, his oracular sight and capacity to know the

[75]Richard Onians, *The Origins of European Thought,* p. 96.
[76]Ibid., pp. 103–106.
[77]Eliade, *Shamanism: Archaic Techniques of Ecstasy,* pp. 36, 245.

past and the future. Actually, everyone has magical fingers and skulls, unconscious impulses manifesting themselves in the fingers and in intuition. But the difference is that the healer takes his impulses seriously; he does not see them as symptoms or personal abnormalities. It is difficult for us to believe that the intuitions, fantasies and ideas popping into consciousness are important. Even individuals trained in psychology have trouble taking fantasies seriously. Yet experience indicates that practically every fantasy that appears spontaneously in consciousness is dreamlike and oracular, a signal from the collective unconscious describing its condition. A spontaneous fantasy is never a strictly personal phenomenon but is always partially dreamed up by the situation one is in.

The healer's difficulty is that he does not realize that the skulls are what the godfather calls "cabbages," that is, edible vegetables to give physical and psychic nourishment. The healer always extraverts all of his information. Hence, a medium may see into someone's childhood trauma, perhaps into the future or into the present. But each insight or piece of information is not only descriptive of the "patient's" life, not simply information out of the *unus mundus,* but information which also deals with the healer's personal psychology.

It always seems to the healer that the information is coming out of the blue and that it has no relevance to his personal situation. Nevertheless, the shamanistic or mediumistic function must be eaten—otherwise the healer will become psychologically impoverished. Many healers and mediums lead complicated and disturbed personal lives because they do not integrate into themselves the material they are so energetically able to project onto others.

The Fish

On the fourth floor the doctor is confronted by fish that are frying themselves. They tell him that the godfather is on the fifth floor.

Fish are cold-blooded, live under the water and are only barely visible. An ancient form of vertebrate life, fish represent the origins of man's physical being and psychologically symbolize the beginnings of consciousness. The important carriers of new forms of consciousness were mythologically fish. Christ was a fish.[78] Matsyendranath, who carried the teachings of yoga from Shiva to man, was also a fish.[79]

Dreams of fish indicate an awareness that occurs when ordinary consciousness is dampened, as on drugs, in meditation or in illness. Fish symbolize vague ideas, intuitions and fantasies of which the ordinary conscious mind is barely aware. Jung called the fish "splinter consciousness" or the consciousness of complexes. Semi-conscious plans or plots appearing spontaneously are the work of "fish." The potential and futuristic aspect of fish finds expression in the astrological sign of Pisces, which is derived from fish motions under the surface of water. They cannot be seen but are somehow felt.

The fish also represent physiological movement which is not normally felt but which may be experienced through introspection. When asked to act fish out, people often accentuate the periodic undulations of these animals in dance and relate these motions to sexual activities. Fish dreams also symbolize the undulating periodic motions of the inner body, such as the peristaltic action of the intestines, the undulations of breathing and the heartbeat. Paracelsus' early medical theory that the blood contained Melusinas, or water nixies who are half female and half fish,[80] is probably derived from the pulsatile sensations of blood flow.

The physiology of fish is elucidated by the imagination of one of my students. After seeing an exciting movie the man quietly meditated on his body and noticed the powerful thumping of his heart. At first he thought the heart was simply excited by the movie, but as he focused on the thumping in the heart area the feeling gave rise to the image of a heavy rolling motion. Soon the heavy feeling appeared to be a large fat woman with an enormous stomach, fat face and a dress much too tight. This image disgusted the man, who disliked fat people. Then he saw that this woman ate too much. She devoured emotional situations and got fat on being overly sentimental. He needed to slim her down by restraining his excitement about everything. Then

[78]Jung discusses the fish in great detail in *CW,* Vol. 9, Part II.
[79]Eliade, *Yoga: Immortality and Freedom,* p. 308.
[80]*CW,* Vol. 13, pp. 42ff.

the thumping abated. The night of this insight he dreamed that an enormous fish brought out of the sea was being cut into pieces for cooking and eating. The fish was the sensation and idea of the fat woman. Now he was going to have to digest his insights about her.

The self-frying activity of the fish refers to the manner in which sensations and ideas perpetuate themselves until they reach consciousness. This self-preparing activity is mirrored in tales and legends about fish that offer themselves to fishermen, hoping to be redeemed and made human by giving crucial information to humans. I think of the little fish that Manu found in his hand in Indian mythology and how this fish asked to be thrown into a larger and larger body of water. Finally it was thrown into the seas and became Vishnu, who told of an oncoming deluge.[81] The fish saved mankind from destruction. As a fish, Vishnu symbolizes queasy feelings, small undulations in mood and slight spasms in the body. These feelings become larger and larger in the story and indicate that they amplify or fry themselves until they are ready to be digested by consciousness. In other words, first the fish are slight feelings, then intuitions or moods, and finally comprehensible ideas.

The fish is a dreambody impulse that amplifies itself and asks for a hearing from consciousness; the fish wants interest, concentration and meditation. If this interest is not given, the fish may perseverate in the form of a chronic ailment asking for attention.[82]

The fish might first appear in the physical motion of closing eyelids, tender hand movements, spontaneous yawns, lip movements and slights movements in the back, shoulder and

[81]*Larousse*, p. 362. Vishnu warned Manu of a flood. Manu built his ship just in time and connected it to Vishnu who had become a giant fish with an immense horn.

[82]The Taoist alchemist amplifies his basic instincts or ''generative forces of life,'' namely Mercury and semen. He brings this process to consciousness in the body by using his imagination, culling the essence of the generative force, hauling it up into the ''cauldron'' at the navel, ''cooking'' this essence and transforming it by fires that are regulated by deep breathing. His meditative act analogues the more common alchemical work in which the alchemist catches the *prima materia* in his vessels and cooks it with the help of fires. The interest, emotional excitement and concentration which the alchemist uses to transform body impulses are reflected in the frying process in our tale—except here the fish, or the body, fries itself without any help from the ego.

rib cage area caused by breathing. The therapist may gently amplify these motions by encouraging the "dreamer" to give them more room without asking him to relate verbally what is happening. Simply exercise the fish motions in the body. The result of such gentle amplification is not just increased body sensitivity but also mental nourishment. A spontaneous insight occurs as body processes ebb and flow into new states, bringing discovery and also frequently increased life or peace. Physiological amplification is difficult to describe because nature itself provides the energy for the work. The therapist only assists what is already happening and tries to give events more room. Neither the analyst nor the patient knows what the amplification will lead to. This is the mystery and secret of the work. One waits until events bring their own solutions. Physical well-being and psychological insight often appear together. (See Fig. 34 in which a healing god appears with flowing fish.)

A woman patient suffered from severe pain in her legs. Her prevailing body experience was heaviness in her eyes and chest. To amplify this experience she closed her eyes and lay down on the floor on her back. In her imaginary heaviness, gravity pulled at her back and drew "roots" out of her spine. But suddenly the roots changed as she meditated on them and became clouds that carried her away. Her heaviness disappeared, she opened her eyes and excitedly told me that she could be carried away in her everyday work, she did not have to do everything with her ego. When she got up, the pain in her legs had lessened. Her decrease in pain is an example of following the flow and letting the fish amplify themselves.

The fact that neither the analyst nor the analysand can tell what amplification of fish-like processes will bring emphasizes that the fish are not preparing themselves for the ego but for something else: The fish are for the godfather.

The godfather is a symbol for what don Juan would have called an "ally," "personal power" or the "double." Everyone has a little of this personal power in the body. It is a second intelligence, dreambody wisdom that puts one on the right track, that organizes body states and manifests in the fish what we call heaviness, tiredness, cramps, pains, sexuality and other impulses. But personal power needs to be developed. It needs to

34. The Healer, Asklepios, Apollo and Oceanus.
(Note fish in lower left.)

be fed in order to live and grow. It needs to follow its own fish, its fingers, skulls, and to amplify its motions until it gets a sense of itself, until the body learns about its own ability to bring events to conclusion, closure and consciousness. Personal power feeds itself.

The woman with pain in her legs mentioned earlier needed to let her power out. Every time the body moves spontaneously, dreambody power manifests itself. What the psychologist identifies as the process of individuation in which the Self comes into consciousness, the body analyst must conceive as the growth of personal power, the manifestation of the dreambody in time and space through the growing consciousness of the body.

At a certain point individuation comes to a halt without body consciousness, just as the growth of personal power is inhibited by lack of intellectual insight into the nature of unconscious processes. The story of the coupling between intelligence and personal power must wait for another chapter. For the moment let me summarize by saying that strong body impulses and diseases are the beginnings of personal power.

Godfather's Secret

Returning to the fairy tale once again, we find the doctor on the fifth floor peeping through the keyhole of his godfather's door. All that our doctor has seen until now has not especially surprised him. As a magical healer he is relatively familiar with body powers and intuition. But now, looking through the keyhole, he sees a picture that surprises him in spite of his abilities. The godfather has horns and his body is covered by a sheet so that he cannot be seen.

What does it mean to hide the body? When there is no body, there is nobody and nothing behind life's events. Where do we find events without anybody behind them, which are not caused and which just simply appear to happen? One area, of course, is a synchronicity. There one dreams or fantasies about something and then, boom, right there in front of one's nose the dream action becomes real. Who caused it? How did it happen? There was apparently no cause. At best, we can only formulate a connecting factor between synchronistic events in terms of meaning.

Another area in which there seems to be no apparent cause for actions is physiology. Often without any particular reason, people are plagued by the strangest symptoms. There is a strong tendency to create a psychological cause for physical illnesses or to locate chemical abnormalities at the root of troubles. But even when we uproot these causes, many illnesses are still not cured. A mysterious X factor is then postulated at the basis of the life process.

The godfather appears not only in synchronicity and symptoms but also in active imagination and meditation. For example, spontaneous visions occurring during breathing meditation lead to typical descriptions of the breathing process as a door that opens and closes without anyone doing the opening and closing.[83] Breathing meditation discloses an absolutely shocking reality: A door opens and closes in the throat area and yet no one is there. Who is doing it? Truly we all live in godfather's house. There is a mysterious spirit behind life and death. The first time I met the swinging door in meditation I was truly shocked and terrified.

Synchronicity, physiology, meditation and quantum physics all manifest a mysterious uncertainty. Bohr generalized physics' uncertainty principle in biology. He said that if we inspect the life process too closely then we destroy it, much as electron processes can be disturbed by experimentation aimed at producing classical information about how, when, why and exactly where.

The reasons for godfather's hiding and his apparently unexplainable behavior do not lie simply in the essence of his own nature. We must realize that the man who is looking at him is someone living in the rational everyday classical world, in an ordinary state of mind. We know that in physics and psychology the observer has an immense effect on the observed. In physics the observer disturbs and participates in the processes. In psychology he can even destroy a fantasy he is looking at.

Synchronicity, parapsychology, magical healing, mediumistic behavior, astral and subtle bodies are descriptions of partially hidden realities which appear uncertain because of the distance between consciousness and the processes it is studying. Getting

[83]Shunryu Suzuki, *Zen Mind, Beginner's Mind*, p. 29.

close to the life process and still not relating to it with ultimate respect and seriousness can be destructive. One recalls don Juan's warning to Castaneda, who did not trust the spontaneity of his own vision:

> That branch was a real animal and it was alive at the moment power touched it. Since what kept it alive was power, the trick was, like in dreaming to sustain the sight of it. . . . Power was a devastating force that could easily lead to one's death and had to be done systematically, but always with great care. He said that properly I should have sustained the sight of the live monster for a while longer. In a controlled fashion, without losing my mind or becoming deranged with excitation or fear, I should have striven to stop the world.[84]

Insensitive egos that rigidly hold to the chronological world of cause and effect can easily destroy psychic and somatic processes. The sensitivity and vulnerability of the godfather in the uncertainty principles constellated by rational observers are described not only in the sciences but also by mythology. In the story of Psyche and her nightly lover Eros, he begged her not to turn on the light to see who he was. But Psyche could not resist wanting to know him and so she betrayed her lover's request, turned on the light and had to suffer the trials of life. The story of Melusine is similar.[85] Like our godfather, she was a water goddess, who according to legend saved Count Raymond from disaster. Her only request was that he not look at her on Saturdays. Of course, he could not resist. He saw that his lovely savior was not simply the beautiful woman he had married but a water nixie. Above she was Melusine, but below she was a serpent, snake or fish! In shock and terror she disappeared, and disaster reigned for many centuries on the family they had produced.

In these tales we find amplification of the idea that one should not look too early at a process that is trying to unravel itself. The soul is very sensitive to the rational world in which we live; its sensitivity is easily and frequently attacked by the ego itself. I notice this constantly in my work. As soon as people begin to follow a body process, they inevitably ask in the

[84]Carlos Castaneda, *Journey to Ixtlan*, p. 133.
[85]Barbara Picard, *French Legends, Tales and Fairy Stories*, p. 101.

beginning: But what is this going to lead to? Where is the instant information? What is the sense of following motions which seem to have no sense? Where is the excitement? How long do I have to wait for something to happen?

The ego, which has ruled over its many processes, has difficulty believing or trusting that something important is trying to take over the body and that something new may in fact result from letting the body or fantasy world flow. Questions about the meaning of the process are not incorrect; they may simply be timed wrong. When asked too early, they destroy what is trying to happen. Body processes rarely reach completion or closure because the ego is uninformed and unaware of their sensitive nature.

What happens when the godfather gets angry at the ego, which wants to know too much too early and interrupts the process? The body at first hides itself. Synchronicities appear along with strange unsolvable illnesses and funny accidents. Later, snakes and angry animals appear in dreams. Like a child, the godfather does not realize that anger directed at the ego is self-destructive. Biological life readily enters onto a crash course and destroys itself. In the end, a type of animal suicide occurs. The horse that threw itself out of the window in Jung's discussion of the dreams of a girl suffering from a somatic illness symbolizes the final stages of a self-destructive biological process.[86] It is dangerous to inhibit biological processes by doubting their significance or trying to understand them before they have completely manifested themselves.

The Horns

Amplification of the horned aspect of the water god gives us additional insight into the functioning of the dreambody. In ancient Europe horns were thought to be outgrowths of the brain.[87] The word for horn has the same etymological basis as the word for cerebrum.[88] Hence, one can say that the horned god is "the mind" of the body, just as the stomach or solar plexus area has always been regarded in India as the second mind.[89]

[86]*CW*, Vol. 16, pp. 158ff.
[87]Richard Onians, *The Origins of European Thought*, p. 285.
[88]Ibid., pp. 237–239.
[89]John Mumford, *Psychosomatic Yoga*, p. 43.

Horns were connected with power and fertility in old Europe. A woman, for example, could give a man horns by sleeping with him.[90] Anyone who has been "horny" knows that that body instinct can seek goals autonomously. These goals may be related to looseness, love, just being, getting out of the head, etc. Pictures of Chinese couples making love (Fig. 35) were not considered images of gross sexual satisfaction, since sexuality in ancient China was related to the unification of yin and yang. The horn symbolizes the drive for completion, wholeness and congruence in a general sense.

The early Christians forbade anyone to drink wine from a horn unless it was first blessed.[91] Pan, the most famous Greek

[90]Onians, *Origins of European Thought,* p. 239.
[91]Ibid., p. 241.

35. The Lovers

horned god, died according to legend when Christ was born.
Here we see that Christ, symbol of the god of consciousness,
supplanted Pan who was the earlier power of the unconscious.
Many of the original deities were horned. The Phoenician wind
god El, from the ancient middle east, and the bull-headed gods
of Egypt are examples. In fact, El governed the flow of rivers,
controlled time and was called the Father of Men.[92] The control
of time and flow emphasizes that the inner timing and self-
governing control of body processes is symbolized by the
godfather.

Eliade reports that one of India's most ancient statues, dating
from about 2500 b.c., portrays a horned deity sitting in lotus
posture with animals at his side.[93] The modern interpretation is
that he is Shiva sitting in lotus position, mastering the animal instincts. But this Shiva already is an "animal" instinct. In other
words, in meditation when the ego is relaxed the Self masters
itself. The body masters itself.

Mercury, Yama, Pan, Wotan, and now the horned deity, are
different aspects of the power of the dreambody, the old mind
which has been repressed with the rise of modern life.

There are many situations in which the conscious mind may
be set aside and in which the dreambody's personal power
brings events to a safe conclusion. I remember a man coming
down from the final stages of a drug trip whose body wanted to
rip itself apart. Actually he only scratched himself in an apparent effort, so as it turned out he did shamanistic surgery on
his abdominal region in order to remove what finally appeared
to be an animal. I was also familiar with the case of a shy and introverted man who finally let himself loose. He wanted to kill
someone, but in the last minute only shook the person. If
trusted, the body cares for itself.

The one mythological figure having most of our godfather's
attributes is the river god of ancient Greece, Achelous. This
figure was considered to be more powerful than the great
Oceanus, "the origin of everything who begot the seas and the
streams, springs and fountains."[94] Often Achelous is pictured
with a bull's horns (Fig. 36). Achelous is reputed to have lost

[92]*Larousse*, pp. 43, 44, 74, 75.
[93]Eliade, *Yoga: Immortality and Freedom*, p. 355.
[94]Kerényi, *Gods of the Greeks*, p. 65.

36.
*Achelous
and
Hercules*

one of his horns in his battle with Hercules, and later this horn became the horn of plenty. The blood that came from the horn created the Sirens, those half-female, half-bird beings who foretold the future. The lower half of Achelous' body is pictured as a serpent-fish, like that of Melusine.

What is so vulnerable and special about the serpentine body? The wave-like configuration of the fish or snake represents fluidity, periodic motion, rhythm and mobility. Wave motion is the opposite of linearity, inflexibility and rigidity. Wave-like motions disturb linear behavior. We find powerful expressions in our language that reflect this: "That really shook me up," or "That person really needs a shaking," or "Shake that out of him." Don Juan tells Castaneda that shivers running up and down the back indicate that the ally is present. Personal power or the Self make one vibrate. We have all witnessed how rhythmical actions of the lips, mouth and chest often precede the breakdown of persona and the outpouring of emotion.

Rhythm and vibration are often experienced as potentially dangerous because rhythm reduces ego control over life. The dreambody often appears in dreams of rigid people as a vibration, threatening chaos, or a temporary and often embarrassing breakdown. Rigidity often hides the simplest and most common humble truths and feelings. The more tenaciously one holds to consciousness, the more uncertain and unstable one feels. It seems as if only the one in contact with the rhythmical and horned god is safe in our world.

This horned god image goes back at least to Paleolithic times. Figure 37a shows a cave drawing from around the 4th century portraying shamanic deities for whom a name still exists. He was called Cernunnos or "The Horned one, Lord of all the Stags."[95] Later he was associated with Pan whose bag of coins expresses his function of provider (Fig. 37b). Apparently he was a god of prosperity and good fortune in ancient Rome, as he had been for early hunters.

Pan then seems to have been integrated into the healing god Asklepios, who is pictured with horns and serpent (Fig. 38). We notice a discrepancy between the angry demon our god-father seems to be and the more or less beneficent Cernnunos figure from which Asklepios may have been derived. Certainly

[95]John Sharkey, *Celtic Mysteries*, pp. 84, 85.

37a.
Cave Drawing of
Healing Stag God

37b.
Pan as Provider

the circumstances in our tale partially account for the godfather's nasty mood. The doctor is hopelessly cut off from
his dreambody powers. These amplifications indicate that
the Godfather—that is, disease and body behavior—depends
strongly on the cultural history of a given individual. We cannot understand the body completely without taking history and
culture into account. A long personal or cultural history that has
repressed the pagan gods encourages illness.

At this time the godfather is raging against the tyranny of rational consciousness. I see this constantly in my practice in the
most unforgettable forms. As soon as people let their bodies express themselves, violent aggression often appears at first.

In any given situation, the therapist has to determine how
much temporary disorder he can tolerate. The history of the
people one works with needs to be reviewed. Are their overall
processes convergent or will they diverge into chaotic out-
breaks which may no longer be self-centering? Sometimes

38. *Pan as Asklepios*

dreams indicate that it would be wiser to avoid a psychotic out-break in which parts can no longer be fitted together. Processes typified by weak convergences can rarely be tolerated in private practice and require treatment and research elsewhere.[96]

However, the vast majority of processes (including many so-called schizophrenic reactions) are quickly convergent. The godfather's rage turns out to be only his repressed limited anger against misunderstanding and insensitivity.

In my experience, if both analysand and analyst remain in a preprogrammed doctor-patient framework, their work will not include the godfather and the body will not be deeply touched. If both doctor and patient try to stay "above water," neither changes much and both secretly wait for the opportunity to be relieved. Living with the body means being one with the Self. The dreambody or personal power is the basis of any relationship with a deep foundation. This is probably why Jung used the pictures of the alchemical opus in which both the alchemist and his apprentice bathe together in the same water as a portrayal of human relationship:[97] two fluid people, changing together (Fig. 39).

This fairy tale demonstrates how archetypal stories are able to enrich the theory of body work. The fish, for example, portrays the body's own tendency to amplify itself in order to nourish the development of personal power. The water god himself is a symbol of all dreambody processes. Hence we must assume that the body nourishes the body if given a chance to do so. The relationship of the fairy tale physician to the spirit of life shows us that prevailing intellectual attitudes cannot grasp the nature of the dreambody. The body is its own explanation. If conscious attitudes toward irrational behavior change, then the truth of the amplifications around the horned body spirit will be realized: The body has its own mind, the dreambody which organizes Life.

---

[96]The Laing clinic case of Mary Barnes is discussed in Boyers and Ortill, eds., *R.D. Laing and Anti-Psychiatry.* She herself states that there are psychotic states with temporarily divergent characteristics which automatically come together if left to themselves.

[97]These pictures come from Stanislaus Klossowski de Rola, *The Art of Alchemy* (plates 41, 42). Jung discusses such pictures and their relationship to the contact between analysand and analyst in his article "The Transference," *CW*, Vol. 16.

39. Fluidity and Change in Relationships

These three fairy tales have portrayed the blocked and pre-
carious course of physicians who, because of their preoccupation with healing, did not recognize the total nature of the spirit
of life or its drive for individuation. Since this spirit, the dreambody, is related to healing only secondarily, a transformation of
a consciousness that focuses only on healing must occur before
people can begin to learn from their illnesses and individuate.

Chapter 4
DREAMBODY AND
INDIVIDUATION

In Chapter 3 I chose fairy tales dealing with healing motifs because body consciousness most frequently awakens with illness. However, we must look elsewhere for images of heroes who not only contact body gods but also use their powers to change real life. The following two tales portray how the dreambody's serpent power is used to transform everyday reality.

THE THREE SNAKE LEAVES

This story is particularly significant because it shows how changes in consciousness can take place and why some transformations fail. My rendition of the tale[1] follows:

> Once a poor man's son left home to earn his living. He enlisted in the army of a king who was in the midst of defending his empire. The boy soon became famous for his heroic acts, arousing his men to battle even when their commander was killed and defeat threatened. After the war the king gave the boy all he wanted. Later, the hero fell in love with the king's beautiful daughter, who was a bit strange because she would only marry a man who promised to bury himself with her if she died first. "What use would his life be to him if he lived?" she asked. She would follow *him* to the grave, in case *he* happened to die first.
>
> The woman became ill and died and, alas, the brave soldier was buried with her in a vault which had only enough provisions for him to live a short time. While sitting in the vault, he saw a snake approaching the body of his dead lady. "Not while I live!" he exclaimed, as he drew his sword and cut the snake into three pieces.

[1]*Grimm's Fairy Tales,* no. 16.

Shortly afterward another snake came but left when it saw the first. It returned with three green leaves which it laid on the first snake and brought it back to life. The hero took the leaves, put them on the eyes and mouth of his dead wife and brought her back to life. But she was worse than before.

While they were returning by boat to visit the hero's old father, the lady became attracted to the captain and together they threw the hero overboard in his sleep. But his trusty servant saw the terrible act, fished up the dead body and restored it to life again with the three leaves that had been preserved upon his master's request. When the king heard of the wickedness of his daughter, he had her executed.

In this tale we find the following symbols: marriage, the hero, the princess, the vault, snakes, the sword, the leaves, rebirth and the motif of betrayal, each of which I want to investigate.

Marriage

The roots of marriage have long been forgotten in our world, where marriage is often experienced as an institution or authority that hinders freedom and must be rebelled against. In the ancient world marriage had other connotations. Richard Onians, for example, discusses ancient associations to the ring and marriage.[2] In ancient Europe the ring was connected with the head and knee, as well as with the finger, and represented bondage throughout all time. The same idea appears in ancient Slavic marriage and burial ceremonies in which both partners agree voluntarily to bury themselves if the other partner dies first. Many legends, including the present tale, have their basis in such archaic traditions.[3]

Why is marriage so binding in these ancient customs? On the most superficial level the common tendency to pray for the death of a partner as a solution to the apparently insolvable

[2]Richard Onians, *The Origins of European Thought About the Body, the Mind, the Soul, the World, Time and Fate*, p. 448.
[3]A Slavonic tale goes like this: The legendary hero Potok-Mikhailo-Ivanovisch took an oath with his wife that whoever should die first after their marriage the partner still alive would commit suicide. Potok's wife died shortly thereafter, and he had himself buried alive with her. "At midnight all monster reptiles gathered around him and then came the great Serpent who burned with a flame of fire. With his sharp sabre Potok killed the Serpent, cut off his head and with the head and blood annointed the body of his wife. She immediately came to life again. They both lived to a great age, but Potok died before his wife and so she was buried alive with him in the dark earth." *New Larousse Encyclopedia of Mythology*, p. 287.

marriage conflict was apparently felt even thousands of years ago and was compensated for by the life and death contract of the marriage bond. Dreams and fantasies of people caught in marriage conflicts often picture the murder and death of their partners.

The total commitment of the ancient marriage contract and its rulership over life and death are also based on a psychological reality: One's partner is a part of oneself; hence it is not possible to divorce oneself, because one lives and dies with one's problems. Oriental philosophy stresses that if problems are not worked out in the reality of this life, they are carried into death and the next life.

Thus psychologically, marriage appears not just as a commitment to an outer partner but as bondage to oneself, to one's own reality, to time and cultural demands. Without the marriage bond and associated guilt feelings, the tendency to avoid inner and outer reality would prevail. A commitment to a partner necessitates working out conflicts. Outer partners, of course, are—in one sense at least—easier to split off and divorce. But not working out problems with an outer partner mirrors the tendency of divorcing inner conflicts as well. Marriage therefore symbolizes, among other things, the conscious commitment to suffer through inner conflicts and to try and transform outer relationships.

The princess' request that her partner be buried alive if she dies first and her willingness to do the same in the reversed case are archetypal processes which beg the ego to commit itself totally to the development of the personality.

The Hero

The hero is a frequently occurring dream symbol in both men's and women's dreams. He is a fighter for the fatherland as in our tale; he is the one who upholds ethical codes and cultural ideas. He symbolizes consciousness and the strength that defends principles in all circumstances.

His negative characteristics are implicit in his way of being. Because of his impeccable ability to uphold consciousness, he tends to be too strong. Hence his feeling and his relationship to the feminine are often disturbed. The unconscious inevitably looms up against the bulwark of his consciousness in the form of some terrible dragon, whale, leviathan or serpent. In real life, a man characterized by a hero's lack of sensitivity and eros is difficult to live with. His feminine side, his wife, often appears in dreams as a terrible witch who is betraying him. Heroic people are often disturbed by feelings that no one loves them and by paranoid types of betrayal fantasies, because they betray their feelings by being strong and berating sensitivity.

Psychologically, the hero symbolizes energy associated with the voluntary bodily activities, energy to accomplish tasks that require training and a firm belief in principles. When he turns negative in dreams, this energy becomes compulsive. Life becomes a humorless, serious struggle to uphold outmoded principles, cultural ideas, and personal obligations.

The Princess

The princess' character is revealed in her fear of dying. Our tale also tells us of her beauty. Her magnificence and the fact that she is the princess of a kingdom indicate that she is a feminine collective ideal of a given *zeitgeist*. She conforms to the given requirements for feminine behavior: she is pretty, says the right things at the right time, is a fine hostess, is vain about her appearance, etc. She symbolizes conventional ideals about the correct way to behave.

Her fears about death turn out to be correct intuitions. Death is really coming! Her time is up. The conventional standard feelings in any culture (or individual) are normally short-lived. New forms of relatedness and eros constantly try to come into being. But before an old attitude dies, consciousness is always troubled by the fear of death. The princess is a collective personality which may appear in anyone's dream as a symbol of collective ideals. She represents the fact that one has no relationship to individual timing but is ruled by collective standards. The less individually personal the life that is lived, the less one is one's self, the greater the tendency to project betrayal and superficiality onto one's partner.

The shaman don Juan would call the princess a relative of the "devil's weed."[4] This feminine ally, the secret of heroic vitality, makes a man's fists burn with anger and his feet itch with the

[4]Carlos Castaneda, *The Teachings of Don Juan.* See the reportage of August 23, 1961.

desire to trample others. She is the hero's inspiration, but she lacks heart, objectivity and coolness. She supports activities only if they succeed.

Symbolizing the energy of the voluntary nervous system that has lost contact with the autonomic nervous system—the breath and the heartbeat—she aims at fulfilling cultural purposes no longer personally significant. She creates a cycle in which at first one wants to succeed and be accepted. But the energy necessary to do this exhausts reserves. One knows that the way one is living is wrong and dreams of leaving this "path without a heart," but one can only fantasy the death of negative dream figures. The unconscious identification with these figures appears in consciousness as the fear of real death. But the princess spurs one on to make greater efforts and to be strong and overcome these fears, and so one starts the whole cycle again. If the princess is not uprooted, illness may result.

Changing partners and being betrayed are frequent themes of seriously ill persons. For example, in analysis one cancer patient dreamed that her husband chose a young woman ("whom he needed") to make love to.[5] A man who was dying from a terminal illness dreamed that he found a new partner but that a piece of wood blocked the entrance to her vagina. This dream occurred after he had attempted to contact his body by doing active imagination with the heart and breath. The piece of wood was related, by his associations, to insensitivity.

Although negative partners in dreams refer to feeling problems and eros difficulties, they may also refer to physiological acts that are out of Tao or out of rhythm with the personality's individual nature. These inner partners can be experienced by talking to negative dream figures in imagination. Physiological experiments reveal them too. For example, let us say that you choose to do something. We can test to see if the energy that chose that thing comes from the voluntary nervous system and is a compulsion, or if it comes from the Self. First, mechanically stop yourself from accomplishing the act. Sit quietly or meditate until a peaceful condition is reached. (During the achievement of this peaceful state the impulses to do the act may reappear as fantasies. These fantasies are often associated to "marriage" partners.) In time, however, the strength of

[5]Selma Hyman, "Death-in-Life, Life-in-Death."

doing impulses subsides and you may experience the harmonious rhythm of the autonomic nervous system. The earlier impulses are still there, but now at a distance they appear as senseless compulsions. You experience a split. Something would like to commit certain acts but you lack the ego energy to accomplish them. Only when the energy persists after such an experience is the original act meant, because it is now being powered by what Jung called the Self. However, if the direction of consciousness has truly changed, the act you wanted to accomplish as an "anima or animus possession" of the voluntary nervous system which had become split off from the Self.

Such meditative experiments are important in understanding dreams and dream figures because dreams occur in states of consciousness physiologically similar to meditation.[6] The negative appearance of human figures in dreams refers to the way time pressures appear in a hypometabolic condition. More will be said about this condition shortly.

The Vault

The vault belongs to the same archetype as the hole in the earth, the cave, crevice, the dark door into the other world, the underworld. It is the abode of the dead, the world ruled by the earth goddess Demeter. The cave is not simply the end-station for all who live too much at the surface in their superficiality; the vault is the last turning point, the last station before death. In our tale, the death chamber is the last stop after living with a feminine principle that has run out of energy; it is the place of depression, physical illness, of sinking into the body. In early Europe, the vault or cave was also the seat of healing and the symbol of dream incubation for those in search of healing dreams. In fairy tales the vault is the last station before absolute death; there may yet be a return to life.

People with terminal illness experience the vault as the battlefield for life in a hypometabolic condition of reduced normal awareness, illness and desperation. Dying people often struggle fiercely but silently for their lives in this condition. Only when we follow their dreams, visions and meditations can we perceive the violent struggle against death which is otherwise barely apparent in the sick body lying limply on the bed.

[6]*Biofeedback and Self-Control,* p. 58.

The hero meets the deadly and also life-giving snakes associated with his dead partner in the vault. Some of the possible psychosomatic effects that occur when the vault situation is constellated in everyday relationships can be amplified here. The vault occurs wherever there is intimate spiritual or physical contact between two people. If you love someone, his or her depressions and problems also depress and trouble you because of the feeling participation and unconscious identification with the life process of the other person. One experiences the problems of the loved one in dreams and in physiological phenomena.

Unconscious problems not only manifest themselves in the psyches and bodies of human beings but also vibrate the inorganic world in the form of synchronicities. The growing, unintegrated animus or male power of young girls notoriously appears in poltergeist phenomena[7] just as the unrealized conflicts and aggressions of gentle people often appear in brutal, even catastrophic accidents occurring near them. The ability of the psyche to appear in material synchronicities seems to indicate that the evolution of the material events depends on man's ability to deal with his body sensations and dreams. If one person can get himself into Tao, a dry region may even suddenly be rained on.[8]

The Snake Archetype

Entrance into the vault and the murder and rebirth of the snake present us with one of the most mysterious and challenging phenomena of psychology: the involuntary nervous system. When a psychological problem has slipped from the normal range of voluntary control, the ability to do body work and active imagination becomes critical because then imagination is our only method of coming to grips with difficulties that are no longer or never were conscious. Addictions to smoking, drinking and other drugs, as well as nervousness, tremor, and slowly degenerating diseases that do not create noticeable symptoms at first (e.g., multiple sclerosis and cancer) are among

[7]Parapsychological and paraphysiological phenomena are described in William Blatty, *The Exorcist.*
[8]Jung tells the "rainmaker story," which he heard from Richard Wilhelm, in *CW,* Vol. 14, p. 419, fn. 211.

the problems met in the vault. The snake is a symbol of deeply rooted somatic and psychological processes.

The biological or zoological properties of snakes are responsible for many mythical projections. The snake lives in water, in trees and on land. When it is poisonous, its venom contains both poison and a sort of anti-poison, a substance which counteracts its lethal effects. The snake has a characteristic vibratory locomotion and changes its skin periodically. It appears in myths derived from its pulsatile and periodic nature. Originally the serpent was connected with the sun and was ruler of the world for the Egyptians and Druids.[9] The snake appears as ruler of nature and as god of thunder and rain in China and Japan.[10]

The snake has many physiological associations. The Kundalini is the Indian term for the energy of the "coiled one" sleeping at the base of the spine which suddenly shoots up the *shushuma* (spinal column) when awakened through meditation and concentration[11] (Fig. 40). Spasmodic vibrations and sudden shivers and shakes were also connected to snakes in early European thought.[12] The backbone was also considered to be the location of the "genius" or soul of the individual,[13] an idea we can readily understand when we look at the anatomy of the spinal column (Fig. 41). Many legends also reveal the serpentine pulsatile aspect of breathing. In some, snakes live in the throat or come out of the mouth when people sleep.[14] The connection of snakes to physical life appears in Germanic legends about household snakes. Snakes under a house are attached to the people living in the house. If one of the snakes suffers or dies, this means misfortune for the individual related to that snake.[15]

Snakes also symbolize measure and boundaries. The serpent Oceanus and the famous Serpent of Midgard[16] in Germanic mythology encircled the world (Fig. 42). The Greek gods

[9]M.O. Howey, *The Encircled Serpent.*
[10]*Larousse,* p. 409.
[11]Mircea Eliade, *Yoga: Immortality and Freedom,* pp. 246–249.
[12]Onians, *Origins of European Thought,* pp. 206–208.
[13]Ibid.
[14]In a Scandinavian tale, a snake comes out of a king's throat while he is sleeping and finds the lost treasures of his kingdom. *Larousse,* p. 277.
[15]Angelo de Gubernatis, *Zoological Mythology, or the Legends of Animals,* p. 393.
[16]John Michell, *The Earth Spirit, Its Ways, Shrines and Mysteries.*

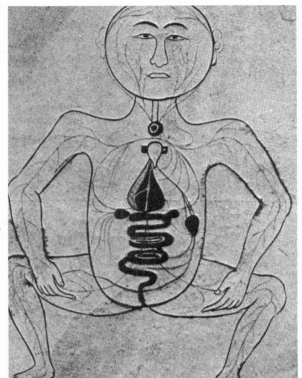

40. *Kundalini,*
    Coiled One

Kronos and Aion are also pictured as serpents, representing time and surviving death.[17]

Boundary snakes like the horrible Serpent of Midgard also have negative, restrictive characteristics and are always accompanied by heroic dragon killers. Indra killed his serpent; St. Patrick, his monster. The thunder god Thor wrestled with the Serpent of Midgard.[18] The serpent killed by Indra in Indian mythology was a monster who held back the waters which were his wives, the flow of nature. Only when he was overcome could the waters flow again into the seas.[19]

The snake symbolizes limits, the border of awareness and hence the border to the unconscious. The evil snake sym-

[17]Marie-Louise von Franz, *Time.*
[18]Howey, *The Encircled Serpent.*
[19]de Gubernatis, *Zoological Mythology,* p. 406.

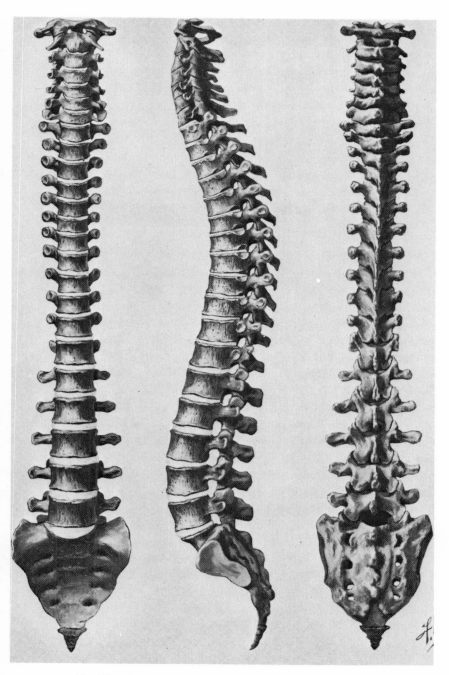

41. The Serpentine Character of Spinal Column

42. The Encircling Serpent of Midgard

bolizes a rigidity that keeps life itself from flowing. In body work the limits of consciousness often appear as shivering or shaking, which is terrifying because it loosens up rigidity and opens the way for uncontrolled flow and hence unpredictableness. The restrictive serpent lying at the gates of the source of flow, or life, is overcome by suffering through these vibrations. Above all, the "hero" must not be afraid of the physical vortices.

The eternal aspect of the snake and its openness to time, life and flow are found in the beneficent feature of Mertseger, the Friend of Silence, who coils up and watches over graves in Egypt.[20] Greece has similar serpents of the dead.[21] Snakes symbolize the vibration of vegetative states, the flow and rhythm of hypometabolic processes that occur during meditation and dreaming and that feel like death (in the positive sense of transcending time).

The two aspects of the snake—its poison and anti-poison, its time and timeless quality—often appear as two aspects of one archetype. The Persians used two snakes to symbolize "long" time and eternal time.[22] There are two snake-like conduits in the Indian subtle body, the Pingala and Ida, which represent the moon and sun, respectively, and symbolize the quiet energy and the passionate body energy closely connected to involuntary and voluntary nervous rhythms (Fig. 43). These serpent conduits in the body are imagined to be silver and red in color.

Snakes are often shown climbing the world tree, which is sometimes surmounted by two fruits, the moon and the sun (Fig. 44). The two snakes wound on a tree branch or staff are a symbol today for healing. Still used by European apothecaries, this is the so-called caduceus, Mercury's staff, which harmonized two fighting snakes (Fig. 45). The caduceus is derived or at least related to the myth of the European healer, Asklepios,[23] who is often pictured with an arm, tree, branch or staff on which a snake is curled (Figs. 46 and 47). According to legend, the snake is Asklepios' tutor, who gave him the healing potions.[24] The connection between the harmony of the two

[20]*Larousse,* p. 41.
[21]Onians, *Origins of European Thought,* p. 207.
[22]von Franz, *Time.*
[23]Jan Schouten, *The Rod and Serpent of Asklepios,* pp. 91, 187.
[24]Ibid., Chapters 1, 2.

*43. The Pingala
and the Ida, Solar
and Lunar Energy
Channels*

44. The Sun and Moon Fruits

FRO BEN,

45. The Caduceus, Mercury's Staff

snakes and the life process is pictured clearly by Mercury or
Hermes, as keeper of the process,[25] standing in the middle of a
tree with his staff entwined by two serpents (Fig. 30).

The body experiences that have two opposing internal body
rhythms find their anatomical equivalent in the different nervous systems. There are two sides of the brain—one responsible for linear rational thinking and one for timeless thought.[26]
There is the autonomic response, which would correspond to
unconscious behavior, and the voluntary nervous system,
which is more closely related to the personal unconscious or
consciousness.

The classical definition of autonomic responses and their in-
dependence from consciousness is no longer valid because

[25]Roger Cook, *The Tree of Life, Symbol of the Center*, p. 112.
[26]Robert Ornstein, ed., *The Nature of Human Consciousness*, p. 87.

46. *Three Images of Asklepios with Snakes*

47. Asklepios with Snake on Arm

yogis and people trained in biofeedback techniques can control some autonomic responses such as heart rate, blood pressure, temperature variations in the skin and rate of blood flow through different parts of the body.[27]

Still another duality exists in the nervous system: the ergo-dynamic system is responsible for sexuality, work and creativity, and the endophylactic-tropic system for restoration and maintenance of body organs. The first is related to doing and the second to maintenance and the creation of energy.

In practice, the interpretation of the snakes depends largely on a given conscious life situation and the details of the dream situation. Negative angry snakes often symbolize the autonomic nervous system or the Self which has become angry at the ego for not relating to the deeper reaches of the personality. Snake fights, or the battle between the snake and an animal with higher consciousness such as a cat, often refer to tensions between the autonomic and voluntary nervous systems.

The most obvious manifestation of the relationship between the two snakes or between autonomic and voluntary activity can be discovered in breathing, which is controlled both by autonomic functioning—as in sleep—and also by voluntary willing—as in speaking. The battle between the snakes or between a primal creature and a more conscious animal manifests in shallow breathing, irregular rhythm and lack of coordination between the voice and the breath. The two systems are in harmony when talking, other vocal sounds and breathing are in accord.

Thus snakes symbolize the life process, autonomous thoughts and spontaneous body experiences. They symbolize limits and the boundaries of consciousness. Snakes have dual characteristics; they are both poisonous and curative. They relate to the personal unconscious or fantasy life close to our voluntary disposal and yet they are the gates to autonomic mindlessness.

I suspect that no amount of scholarly research suffices to give one a feeling for the essence of snakes. I therefore recommend an experiential method for contacting snakes:

Sit quietly and do nothing. After a few minutes begin to count exhalations of breath. Count 1, 2, 3, etc., with each ex-

[27] *Biofeedback and Self-Control.* The various autonomic controls are described in the first part of this text.

halation to 10. Then repeat. After a few minutes or so, your counting will be disturbed by some physical motion or internal dialogue. At this point, people who have not developed the capacity to concentrate on imagination and those who are simply overworked and tired will fall asleep. But if awareness is sharpened, then one will catch a fantasy or inner dialogue which disturbs counting. If one is aware of what is happening, one can note this dialogue and make it conscious, and also note how this inner conversation or fantasy affects breathing.

Two types of snake-like phenomena may be noted in this experiment. The first snake is the inner dialogue that disturbs one's attention. This snake, which catches one's inner eye when one is meditating (in the vault), is fantasy. It also has physiological significance. If the first snake is studied and worked through and the complex it symbolizes worked out, then one comes to a second snake—a sort of mindless, spaceless, timeless, feeling in which one feels very much at peace and regenerated. The first snake—let us call it for short "doing" or "time"—is the root of complexes. Mythologically, the first snake encircles the earth, possesses and limits one in a sort of cyclical thought pattern. The first snake is not simply evil. It is the origin of consciousness and its perseveration. It keeps the world going and is typically related to existential problems, such as calculating when to pay the bills, planning what to do next, protecting against disaster and fate. The second snake symbolizes timelessness, a gestaltless feeling of traversing into dimensionlessness. Time, the first snake, becomes deadly when it possesses consciousness, choking life and flow by blindly driving to solve existential concerns. The second snake, by contrast, is related to subtle body or out-of-body experience.

The first snake is the origin of what don Juan calls "doing," or the drive responsible for upholding cultural ideals and consciousness. The first snake, though rooted in unconscious phenomena, is the origin of culture and conventional feeling; it is therefore often the evil keeper of women forced to be the snakes' lovers in legends.[28]

In India liberation and wisdom are described as cutting through the physiological reactions of the first snake.[29] In the

[28]de Gubernatis, *Zoological Mythology,* pp. 394–396.

[29]According to an ancient Indian text, "gathering . . . is the characteristic

West, psychological development is mainly connected to the information which is wrapped up with the consciousness of dream figures such as the anima. But cutting the snake down at the instinctive level only will not necessarily transform one's relationship to the world, just as transforming one's feelings and conventionality will not always correspond with physiological transformation. Work on the snake and its partner, the princess, must go hand in hand. Even in the East simply cutting down the first snake and achieving stillness is not considered the highest goal. "The stillness in stillness is not the real stillness. Only when there is stillness in movement can the spiritual rhythm appear which pervades heaven and earth," says a Taoist text.[30]

The limiting snake is such a bother that as soon as it is done away with there is a tendency to feel that only the second snake ("being," the mindless rhythm of vegetative life) is god. Since the first snake is bound with consciously alterable attitudes, it may be typified as the "mind," although this designation is not quite correct. The mind-body spirit we hear so much about today is a manifestation of the conflict between the two snakes. Many people who discover body work suffer an apparently archetypal problem of thinking that the body is the sole guide and wants to avoid any intellectual formulation of somatic experiences. This problem apparently has historical roots.[31]

The Sword

The application of active imagination to processes in the vault is symbolized by the hero's use of the sword. Understanding the sword will help us handle the first snake.

An extension of the arm, the sword is part of the same archetype that governs staffs, magical rods, clubs, defense and attack

---

quality of attention and *cutting off* [emphasis added] is the characteristic quality of wisdom." Nyanaponika Thera, *The Heart of Buddhist Meditation,* p. 185.

[30]Fritjof Capra, *The Tao of Physics,* p. 205.

[31]Heinrich Zimmer (*Philosophies of India,* Chapter 1) describes India's ancient conflict between collecting information about events and knowing through direct transformation. Real knowledge is like a lion which was fated to be brought up by goats (the intellect) but which rediscovered itself later with the help of a powerful father lion.

weapons. The sword represents the power of the shaman, hero, priest and warrior.[32] In our tale the sword is used to govern the snake world, the world of subtle energies.

Handling subtle energies is important in the development of body awareness and the achievement of individuation. One finds the battle with subtle energies in the story of Buddha's enlightenment, in his warrior-like determination to meditate under the fig tree and hold his place until Mara, chief of the demons, lost his power.[33] In *The Secret of the Golden Flower* we are advised to return all energies to their original source and warned that failure to do so will result in premature aging and ill health.[34] In Hermetic, Kabbalistic and kundalini yoga traditions, the governing of snake energies is the secret of wisdom and life. In the Hermetic story, Hermes throws down his staff and harmonizes two snakes. In the Kabbala, the initiate must train the green serpent of wisdom to come up the tree of life, staying between two central pillars.[35] In kundalini yoga, the kundalini must be trained to arise in a balanced fashion, between the red and white nervous circuits.[36] Taoistic yoga is also based on the mastery—through breathing—of a subtle energy called mercuriality or vitality.[37] These rituals all try to master serpent energy and use inner concentration, meditation and active imagination on the subtle body responses.

The sword is related to the mastery of an active imagination on the body. Early Germanic legends tell of an interesting relationship between the sword and serpent energies.[38] Each sword originally had its own individual characteristics. Specific swords had names and were inhabited by snakes. The hero who wanted his sword to work well for him had to talk to and win the friendship of the snake that inhabited the sword. He breathed on the snake, talked and cared for it in special ways. The primitive mind sees tools and weapons as animated-

[32]Schouten, *Rod and Serpent of Asklepios,* pp. 40, 41.
[33]*Larousse,* p. 349. Buddha says that the "snake" that must be annihilated is the "thirst for pleasure . . . existence . . . change."
[34]Jill Purce, *The Mystic Spiral: Journey of the Soul,* p. 25.
[35]Ibid.
[36]Ibid., p. 26.
[37]Lu K'uan Yü, *Taoist Yoga.*
[38]K. Saezle, *Tier, Mensch und Symbol,* p. 385.

inspired objects with personalities of their own. The relationship between the serpent and the arm of the healer, his staff or branch was discussed earlier.

The snake in the sword indicates that the weapon which controls the dreambody's subtle energies is not wielded simply at the will of the ego. Control of these energies depends paradoxically on the energies themselves. Manipulating the body without deference to the dreambody does not work. For example, simply telling a nervous person to be calm will not succeed. Nor does giving "correct" information and insight have any effect if the timing of the information is not right. "Timing" is symbolized by the snake living in the sword. The sword is action, while the snake is the "when and how" of the action. Timing is a complex factor related to the personal situation, the collective Tao, body conditions and relationships between people. The sword is a property of the mind and body which knows when and how to cut.

The sword is partially man-made, which means that it can be developed with the use of conscious training. Analysis, for example, develops a psychic sword by continuous work on dreams. In time the ego can even relax and—when the sword is developed—act without thinking.

The sword, which is half-man, half-serpent, half-voluntary, half-involuntary, has many analogues. It appears in yoga, where one must first train the body in the art of moving slowly and mindfully and then the body does the rest. According to the old sages, yoga teaches yoga.[39] A trained body teaches the art of moving in the body. Then a sense of well-being, which one becomes familiar with through the training, does the rest.

The same principle of half-conscious, half-unconscious control operates in meditation too. At first one develops a "Beginner's Mind," to use a Zen phrase.[40] One allows all fantasies to enter into consciousness; then one intensifies or even entertains them. This toleration makes them disappear. Actually what happens is that through the mechanism of feedback the psyche learns how to deal with fantasies. It unconsciously takes note of them and puts them into effect in everyday life without one

[39]Eliade, *Yoga: Immortality and Freedom,* p. 39. "Yoga manifests itself through Yoga."
[40]Shunryu Suzuki, *Zen Mind, Beginner's Mind.*

knowing or realizing how. The analyst consciously integrates the fantasies which the yogi simply tolerates. Consciously deciding to change one's behavior according to the nature of the fantasies that appear in meditation also makes them disappear. They are compensations for unconsciousness which disappear once they are taken seriously. Biofeedback will work according to a similar compensation mechanism.[41] In any case, let us assume for the moment that if symptoms and fantasies are amplified and made conscious they learn to handle themselves as if a magical sword were present.

The Three Snake Leaves

The hero is waiting patiently for the end of life when the first snake approaches his dead wife in the vault. He takes his sword and cuts the aggressive snake into three parts to protect the woman's body. A second snake then appears, departs and returns with three leaves which heal the first snake. Finally, the two snakes go off together, leaving the leaves behind. In a similar tale from the Island of Lesbos baby snakes are dismembered by a heroine protecting her dead lover and the mother snake comes and put them together again.[42]

To understand the snake's rebirth, it is useful to look into the predictions of yoga and alchemy. In India, the kundalini is awakened or reborn and enters the different chakras when impurity, insensitivity and restlessness are overcome. In Taoistic alchemy, when mercury has been tamed and sexuality "stored," flow, rebirth, health and immortality result.

The second snake's arrival symbolizes physiologically the appearance of the hypometabolic condition that occurs when compulsions are mastered. Normally this condition occurs only during sleep. When it takes place in waking life, hypnogogic visions and nirvana-like states result. One feels peaceful. One may even have out-of-body experiences in which normal body sensations are replaced by sleep-like phenomena. One becomes conscious of oneself as a dreamer and sits in Samadhi. The Indian technique of pranayama, the inhibition of breath, is especially aimed at producing such hypometabolic condi-

---

[41]*Biofeedback and Self-Control,* pp. 12–34.
[42]"Die Prinzessin und die Schlange, Inselmärchendes Mittlemeers." Collection: *Die Märchen der Weltliteratur,* p. 22.

tions.[43] The second snake symbolizes another tempo, another rhythm, a sort of timelessness and peace normally foreign to consciousness.

The murder of the first snake (i.e., the taming of compulsion) constellates the kundalini or the second snake. Likewise, energy attached to inhibitions in conscious life appear in new forms when the restrictions are worked through. Many Self symbols appear in dreams when mastery of the first snake has occurred in consciousness. Symmetries, plants, shrubs, flowing water, flowers and fruit are typical dream images of Samadhi. Gilgamesh's prickly bush from the bottom of the sea which brings immortality also fits here. The trees of knowledge and immortality, wheat, bread, god, pregnancy, love and flying also symbolize liberation from time. The harmony implicit in the Buddha's ordered snakes (Fig. 48), contrasting with the ungoverned quality of Medusa's snakes (Fig. 49), is another symbol of mastery over the first snake and the resulting peace in the autonomic nervous system.

The leaves used by the second snake to heal the first are vegetative experiences which regenerate the energies of doing by harmonizing them with autonomic activity. The rebirth of the first snake through the help of the second symbolizes the mysterious process of not-doing, in which existential problems are resolved not by doing but by the dreambody's operating spontaneously.

The Rebirth of the Princess and Betrayal of the Hero

The reader will recall the finale of our tale. The hero puts the leaves on the princess' mouth and eyes and she comes back to life. But later she betrays him for the captain of a ship on which she and the hero are sailing. She and the captain try to kill the hero by throwing him overboard. A servant saves the hero and the King has his daughter killed when he learns about her treachery.

Why such a sad ending to a tale that began so beautifully? The roots of the ending are found already in the beginning. Our strong man heroically defends his nation and even his woman, but he does not focus his attention on her world. His lack of relationship to the feminine makes it possible for his own inner

[43]Eliade, *Yoga: Immortality and Freedom,* pp. 55–57.

48. *Buddha, with Serpent Force Mastered*

49. *Head of Medusa*

femininity to remain too undeveloped and chaotic. Since he remains the hero, his anima—i.e., his feelings for himself—betrays him by falling for the captain, the hero's own shadow which fathers and protects others. The person who heroically binds himself to deeds and who unconsciously identifies with cultural roles performs an act of self-betrayal because the total personality is made up of other components besides paternal heroism. In other words, the hero is simply too heroic. He does things even though he may not have the appropriate feeling or energy required.

The dramatic problem of our tale is that the anima is cut off from her vegetative roots, the snake and its leaves. In becoming cultural beings, we humans lose contact with the vegetative nervous system, just as the world of the primitive ape has slipped into oblivion.

In our fairy tale the hero begins to reattach the anima to the world of plant leaves and snakes. But he fails to complete this work because he focused on his "doing" instinct only in the vault and lost track of his cultural and heroic behavior as soon as he left meditation. He has broken the marriage bond to himself.

This story could have come directly from India, could have described the first part of Buddha's fate or related the symbolism of kundalini yoga. Our tale tells us, in accordance with subtle body theories from all over the world, that dreambody energy is divided into two aspects which I have chosen to call "doing" and "being." The life process depends to some extent on governing these energies.

The hero's job is to uproot doing's compulsion. Then the body does the rest. When new energy is awakened it produces almost indescribable effects. These effects are phenomena of introverted, inner concentration and meditation, which belong to the lonely realm where one confronts the life process on its own terms. An analyst or therapist can barely deal with this realm of the patient which, in the end, can be touched only by the individual himself.

But our tale also gives us a warning: Active imagination coupled with body meditation may create temporary peace and a sense of physical well-being, but it does not solve conflicts with the world and the possessive hold of mundane interests.

Reaching nirvana and engaging in deep meditation are Eastern versions of Western tranquilizers. Coupling inner harmonies with outer obligations must remain a challenge.

THE WHITE SNAKE: TRANSFORMING REALITY

In "The White Snake"[44] the hero succeeds in transforming the woman he loves, and in so doing changes himself as well. The special methods he uses, his relationship to the mysterious white snake and the turmoil he must go through are patterns of *individuation,* of the development of dreambody awareness and of the creation of a relationship with a real living person. My rendition of this beautiful love tale goes as follows:

> Once there was a king who knew all things. But he had the strange habit at mealtimes of being served a covered dish after everyone else had finished eating. Finally his faithful servant could no longer contain his curiosity about the dish, opened it, saw a white snake and ate a little bit of it. Immediately he could hear and understand the voices of animals. At the same time the queen lost her ring, and as suspicion fell upon the servant, he went to look for it and heard a duck admitting that it had eaten the ring. The servant had the duck killed for dinner, retrieved the ring and won his freedom.
>
> As he began his travels he heard fish crying that they were stuck in the reeds. After he put them back into the water, he avoided stepping on ants because they complained that humans and their horses always stepped on them. The hero killed his horse and fed it to baby ravens whose parents had thrown them out of the nest and left them on the ground to starve. Finally, he arrived in another kingdom and bid for the daughter of the foreign king. To win her he must first find the ring she had thrown into the water, then gather together millet seeds she had scattered on the ground and finally fetch an apple from the tree of life. The animals he had previously helped came to his aid. The fish found the ring, the ants put the millet seeds into bags and the ravens got the apple for him while he was lying exhausted in the forest looking for the tree of life. In the end, he shares the apple with the princess, the two fall in love and live happily ever after.

The central mystery in our tale is the white snake. According to Gubernatis:

[44]*Grimm's Fairy Tales,* no. 17.

In Germany, the white serpent (that is the snowy winter) according to popular legend, gives to whoever eats of it, or who is licked by it in the ears, the gift of understanding the language of birds, and of universal knowledge. It is the night of Christmas, that is, in the midst of the snow, that those who are predestined to see marvels can comprehend, in the stables, the language of the cattle, and, in the woods, the language of the birds; according to legend, Charles le Gros, in the night of Christmas, saw heaven and hell open, and was able to recognize his forefathers.[45]

The white snake represents the quiet and sleepiness of winter, the periods when consciousness is lowered and one is open to mediumistic sight. When the king, Charles the Great, recognizes his "forefathers," he is, psychologically speaking, seeing his predecessors, his own earlier incarnations.

At one time the Scandinavians worshipped house snakes, among which the white snake was supposed to be a good spirit.[46] The snakes used by Germanic peoples prior to Christianity to divine the future are relatives of the white snake which gives kings knowledge.[47]

The white serpent is found also in kundalini yoga where knowledge of earlier births is a goal in training.[48] The two nadis, or subtle body channels, through which kundalini energy flows are defined as red and white circuits carrying sun and moon energy, respectively. If the kundalini ascends the red channel, something like a psychosis can result. Gopi Krishna's search for the white serpent in his physiology documents the steady, cool, detached state of mind connected with white serpent processes.[49] In China the white serpent symbolizes wisdom and coolness while the red serpent is related to wild passionate undertakings and drunken states.[50]

Chinese, Indian and Germanic amplifications indicate that the white serpent is related to hypometabolic conditions, which were attributed to the second snake in the Three Snake Leaves

---

[45]de Gubernatis, *Zoological Mythology*, p. 407.
[46]Saezle, *Tier und Mensch, Gottheit und Daemon*, p. 387.
[47]Ibid.
[48]Eliade, *Yoga*, p. 181.
[49]Gopi Krishna, *The Kundalini*.
[50]Rolf Homann, *Die wichtigsten Körpergottheiten*, p. 84, fn. 1. An ancient text tells how the white snake god was killed by a drunken man, embodying a red serpent.

tale. The white snake may be differentiated from its opposite, the red snake, which symbolizes "fired" physiology, compulsion and blind drivenness. The red snake governs the voluntary nervous system without reference to the total condition of the body or psyche.

If the reader wishes to contact the white snake in an experimental way, he can begin by simple meditation on the breath. Secondly, he should gradually create an *asana* of hatha yoga or any physical posture, then punctuate changes in posture by meditation. While performing these different postures, concentrate on letting the body direct the timing and succession of movements. After a while one feels that the body itself directs what is happening. The last stage of the experiment consists in continuing movement at the direction of this inner body guru.

A yogi's meditative movement creates an awareness of the dreambody guide. Any meditative action works equally well (e.g., the Buddhist method of meditative walking).[51] Hatha yoga is especially useful because its body postures are archetypal and because if one meditates long enough, without even knowing hatha yoga, the body automatically performs such postures.[52]

Eliade discusses the final stages of yogic practice in which a white snake effect occurs; one reaches deep concentration, stasis or Samadhi.[53] This stage of yogic activity gives the feeling that one is different from one's body. The yogi in Samadhi experiences himself as a spirit located only relatively in the body. In this state, everything becomes apparent, or according to the *Yoga Sutras,* the "Yogin knows the cries of all creatures."[54]

Thus the white snake symbolizes Samadhi. The previous experiment gives one a hint at this state of mind. "The cries of all creatures" heard in this hypometabolic state are the inner voices or signals of one's own mind and body that appear when internal dialogue and normal consciousness are turned off. This

[51] Walking meditation is described in Nyanoponika, *The Heart of Buddhist Meditation,* pp. 96ff.
[52] I refer the reader again to the old Yogic text which says that yoga teaches yoga (Eliade, *Yoga,* p. 39). In body work, I have frequently been amazed at the ability of persons who are not at all acquainted with yoga to automatically perform the *asanas.* The bends and twists of these postures are definitely archetypal forms which the body tries to fulfill.
[53] Eliade, *Yoga,* pp. 68, 70, 84.
[54] Ibid., p. 85.

state is normally experienced only in dreaming where the animals then symbolize the patterns that appear in the dreamer's inner theater. However, the white snake refers to a consciousness of the dreaming state in which one is fully alert and awake.

There are many ways of reaching Samadhi using the white snake. Shamans use drugs to get there. Don Juan differentiates the white snake from its opposite, a red "snake" connected with force, power and passion.[55] Meditation, hatha yoga or extreme physical exertion cut down the red snake and allow the white one to appear. Exhaustion, illness and dreaming also spontaneously create Samadhi.

The King

Since the king symbolizes rulership of consciousness, a king who eats the white snake represents a divinatory government of conscious life. The servant of such a king is a person who follows dreams, oracles (such as the *I Ching*), body phenomena and synchronicities. Learning to serve the divinatory principle is the first stage of apprenticeship to the unconscious in the *Journey to Ixtlan,* where don Juan asks Castaneda to pay attention to "agreements from the world around us."

But if the servant does not eat the white snake himself, he does not integrate the unconscious. He only admires it from a distance and handles it with intellectual gloves. Synchronicities, agreements and dreams are "out there." The difference between someone who serves the king and someone who eats the king's dinner and then receives the ability to understand the animals himself is the same as the difference between one who listens to his dreams and one who steps into the body in order to experience directly what the dreams are saying.

Jung says in his *Letters* that stepping into dreams and doing active imagination is the second half of analysis, and that without "active imagination" one can never become independent of a psychotherapist.[56]

---

[55]Don Juan gives Castaneda the Devil's Weed (jimson weed) to help him experience the masculine power drive in himself, characterized by the color red. The cool wisdom of the white "smoke" brings heart and insight instead of power.

[56]C.G. Jung, *Letters,* Vol. 1, p. 459.

One serves the king and is not free unless one personally experiences the unconscious. Since animals refer to archetypal processes and images, understanding the language of animals is psychologically equivalent to stepping into the dreambody world and living with dream image and body sensations.

The yogi and his archaic predecessor the shaman characteristically understand the language of animals.[57] The shaman, like the individual doing active imagination, steps into the dream world and actually becomes the animal. Through this becoming he understands and empathizes with animals. Typical shaman animals such as snakes, birds, lizards and bears often refer to states of mind and body in which the individual, once having created the white-snake effect by means of drumming, music and dance, actually becomes an animal. One can also become an animal in a controlled way by imitating dream images or by stepping into feelings and acting out sensations in the body.

The Duck

In Greek, the word for duck is Penelope. Penelope was the woman who was devoted to Odysseus and waited for him. Duck-Penelope came to mean devotion.[58] As soon as the servant eats the white snake the queen's ring falls into the duck's mouth and only the servant knows what has happened to the ring, because only he can hear ducks talk. In other words, the commitment to the king (the queen's ring) has fallen into "devotion," and the servant must kill this devotion by making it conscious. In this way he obtains his freedom.

The process of eating the white snake alters consciousness and enables one to become aware of a special type of devotional dependency. One may have listened to, adored, followed and trained oneself to know the unconscious but still may have never truly experienced it. Only when consciousness is altered through accident, illness or body work can one realize that the previous devotion to the Self was a type of subservient dependency which now inhibits development. This realization is mirrored in our tale by killing the duck.

Killing the duck and eating it refers to integrating projections which one has had onto the Self. This is one of the most difficult projections to overcome because it is so subtle. So much

[57]Eliade, *Yoga,* p. 178.
[58]Kerényi, *Heroes of the Greeks,* p. 321.

energy is invested in admiring dreams and body processes. Much admiration may also be projected onto a great woman or great father figure. One sits quietly and worships the "great mountain" but unconsciously binds oneself to an infantile condition in which the great one is always out there.

Why does the king keep his snake covered so that no one can see what is on the dish? The secret to his method of ruling the kingdom is becoming or experiencing the Atman, knowing that part of oneself which is God. One's own development necessarily keeps this experience from consciousness because if such a powerful condition is discovered too early, the person may lose the desire to continue living in the ordinary world or may become inflated. Long and arduous training is often needed before service to the king may be transformed into active imagination or letting the body flow. Most psychology students first do their service to the king by meticulously learning about the unconscious, discovering how complexes, "power" and numen manifest and how to fit these manifestations together with conscious problems. When this intellectual framework is created, they can let go with controlled abandon and let dreams appear by themselves in the body or fantasy world. Without the intellectual framework, living dreams or body work remain simply an ecstatic experience without integration into life.

Meeting the Fish

Our hero now makes his way through a no-man's-land in which he confronts different animals before finally coming to the kingdom of his bride-to-be. There are various ways to describe the animals the hero meets. Since I am stressing the physiological aspect of symbols, I prefer to emphasize the dreambody experiences and refer secondarily to ordinary psychology, especially since the interpretation of animal symbols from the psychological point of view is already partially known.[59]

The stranded fish crying out for help, as well as other animals the hero meets that are also fighting for their lives, indicate that without the ego *the body is not a self-sustaining system.* Modern biophysics, however, views the body as a homeostatic self-regulating organism. When one is "in" the body, just as when one enters the dream world in active imagination, it

[59]von Franz, *Introduction to the Psychology of Fairy Tales.*

becomes strikingly clear that specific processes in the body and in dreams need to be governed by consciousness.

As discussed earlier, the fish symbolize pulsatile somatic sensations which are potential allies and aids to consciousness. The various tales and legends about fish carrying secrets refer to the fact that the pulsatile fluctuations and spasms in the gut, heart and breath bear important messages. The fish that are stranded in the reeds refer to subliminal (that is, to ordinary consciousness) impulses which will dry out if not propagated or amplified by consciousness. Such propagation may take the form of encouraging fantasies to go on, amplifying and allowing body impulses to become stronger and to continue in their own fluid element. The fish can be saved by amplifying sensations, dream images and fantasies, and generally by fructifying unconscious processes. If the ego does not support or notice fantasy and body life, then it tends to dry up and die. If a fish dies, the organs associated with vibratory signals become exhausted, weakened and ill.

Since fish live in water, helping them back into the water helps an aspect of the personality to remain itself. As a fish one is a dreamer, dancer or inhabitor of the visionary world.

The Ants

As soon as the servant has helped the fish back into the water he hears the ants calling out that they are being stepped on by the horse. Unlike the fish, ants live on land and autonomously create order. In mythology ants play a decisive role in overcoming evil serpents. The hero or heroine in search of immortality appears as an ant before the mother of time, on whose door there is a serpent biting its own tail. The hero who saves the ants from flood and other destruction in fairy tales wins their friendship and is aided in collecting scattered objects.[60]

Ants represent autonomous creative fantasies. Physiologically these fantasies appear as the forces behind itching, twitching, "bugging" feelings, and also scratching motions of the hands and feet. Ants belong to the realm of involuntary autonomic acts not controlled by the ego. These ants are opponents of the "evil serpents," another form of the "first" or "red" snake which becomes destructive to vegetative life when basically voluntary acts and instincts go ungoverned by consciousness.

[60]de Gubernatis, *Zoological Mythology,* pp. 44–46, 47.

The horse, symbol of consciously controlled body movements since earliest time, is ordinary action, an aspect of the "evil serpent," which consciousness may manipulate and tame.[61] When the horses are controlled in yoga, the Purusha or soul appears. If horsepower—the drive to do and to go—is killed, the ants can live, because as long as one is pushing with the ego the itchings of the body are not listened to. The ants crying out for help are autonomous body motions asking protection from insensitivity. The ants' liveliness symbolizes the creativity of spontaneous fantasy in contrast to the ego's plodding directedness.

The Raven

Our hero kills his horse and sacrifices it to the raven children who are lying on the ground, crying out for help. Ravens are related to melancholy, death and the devil.[62] Take a piece of the white snake and become a bird in order to know the raven. Shamans have described people who have become birds, so we have a good idea of the raven-bird experience.[63] As a bird, one flies, is supported by the wind and floats effortlessly without the force of gravity. Birds symbolize out-of-body experiences. The mythical bird Guarda at the top of the yogic tree (which represents the spinal column) symbolizes what happens when the kundalini is constellated. A hypometabolic state comes through working and meditating on the body, and energy transforms from body sensations into a mythical or fantasy bird. The yogi who meditates on his wind, or breath, becomes a bird living in the air. The shaman who enters into trance states has astral or subtle body experiences normally given only to dreamers or individuals close to death.

The raven's parents kick their young out of the nest and let them live or die according to fate. If we apply this characteristic

[61]Horses are connected to the untamed body as a chariot is connected to the driver, soul or Atman. The best known symbol of yoga is yoking—a horse connected to a rider or carriage. The horse is a symbol of culturally driven physiological energies. Horses often run wild in dreams, endangering people and the environment. Cancer patients frequently dream of being run over by horses. We must assume from this symbol that the cancer process itself is a form of unconsciousness or possession of the voluntary nervous system which is, in principle at least, tameable through sensitivity, awareness and controlled "doing."

[62]von Franz, *Introduction to the Psychology of Fairy Tales.*

[63]Mircea Eliade, *Shamanism: Archaic Techniques of Ecstasy,* p. 403.

to dreambody experiences, then the raven symbolizes the abandonment of body experience. Life itself is a raven. We are ejected from the womb, plummeted into life and left to fate. People with negative parent experiences have an excess amount of raven psychology in them. They live like ravens, are overly cautious, afraid and suspicious. A raven-like feeling of abandonment complicates intimate relationships when partners accuse each other of being raven parents and not caring. But the raven crying for help is a dreambody which cannot care for itself. The dreambody calls out for help. Unconsciously, people project their raven problem onto someone else, claiming that others do not care enough. In reality it is one's own innermost center that is crying out for love; only ego consciousness can give this love by focusing on dream messages and body motions.

When the hero kills his horse and feeds it to the ravens, he takes the energy he was using to horsepower himself through life and feeds it to his soul. He inhibits power drives and meditates, becoming a bird. He becomes sensitive to the dreambody (the raven) through having eaten the white snake. He knows that the subtle life of a bird depends entirely on how much energy he gives to inner experiences. When the raven is fed, the individual follows the flow of his fantasies and body movements and knows that the greatest loneliness is the desperation of the Self, unattended by consciousness and in danger of dying. If the raven dies, the experience of the Atman becomes split off from consciousness and/ or is uninspired.

The raven is often related to the devil in myths. If the Self is not cared for and fed, if the subtle body experience is not amplified by consciousness, then it manifests negatively in the form of symptoms and accompanying fears of death. Behind death fears connected to body symptoms is the call of the raven, the soul that has not been fed. Hence a physical symptom is only partially a devil.

The Search for the Princess
When emerging from a state in which one hears the animals and follows their messages, one feels enlightened. Whatever was wrong seems to have been corrected. Now one has animal

friends, personal powers, and all things seem possible. The raven soul is discovered, and a state of nirvana, peace and equilibrium could be attained if desired. At this point one could leave the world, perform magical feats as a shaman or spin from one vision to another. This happens to many yogis after they finish their initiation. They become enlightened and then leave the world, becoming monks, abandoning family life and transforming into mystics. Achieving a certain mastery over their minds and bodies, they enter a condition of eternal love and detachment.

The hero of our tale returns to the human world which is either a new kingdom or the old world in a new perspective, and falls in love with a woman, hoping to prove that he can fulfill her needs.

The interest in concentrating on his partner's needs and fulfilling her requirements is a new and important element. The inability to listen or focus on a partner is a major cause of disturbance in relationships. At a deeper level, this inability indicates a lack of understanding and a lack of relationship to what the partner symbolizes in oneself. Lack of relationship to a real partner refers, above all, to a split in the individual personality.

The Eastern attitude to the feminine, to eros and love is much different from ours. The gods of the East are both masculine and feminine. China pictures yin and yang in sexual conjunction (Fig. 35) just as India visualizes Shiva and Shakti in intercourse.[64,65] Female organs such as the vulva are worshipped as gods in India,[66] and only female priests can help the male initiate to nirvana.[67] Western gods such as Christ, the Holy Ghost or Yahweh are never pictured making love.

In India undeveloped or unconscious femininity is called *Maya*, which is Shakti's first stage before development takes place (Fig. 50). Maya transforms through meditation, yoga or ritualized sexuality. This transformation lifts the domination of time (Fig. 51).

[64]Philip Rawson and Laszlo Legeza, *Tao: The Chinese Philosophy of Time and Change,* plate 45.
[65]Philip Rawson, *Tantra,* plate 38.
[66]Ibid., plates 10 and 11.
[67]Ibid., p. 23.

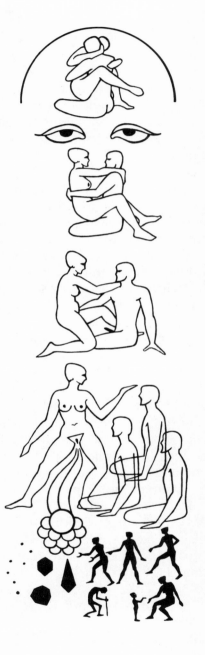

The all-embracing whole of Reality

*Reality divided as the sexual pair,
Shiva and Shakti, within both man
and world, so deeply joined they are
unaware of their differences and
beyond Time*

*The sexual pair become aware of
their distinction*

*The female 'objective' separates
from the male 'subject'*

*The female 'objective' performs Her
dance of illusion, persuading the
male 'subject' he is not one but many,
and generating from Her womb the
world of multiplied objects in what
seems to be a sequence in time*

*'Subjects' perceive a differentiated
reality, seeming to be composed of
separate particles of objective fact,
and live lives that seem to be
extended in time*

50. **The Transformation of Shakti**

51. *Kali as Time*

Feminine imagery is missing in Western religious symbolism.[68] One of the results of this lack of imagery is that Maya, or time stress, is unknown to us as an *inner* phenomenon. We try to fight time by relaxing or taking vacations, not realizing that time is a god, that it is an instinct. Linear time can be relativized only by noting the anima or animus, that is, the doings of everyday life. Doing is relativized through dream work and body awareness.

The princess (Maya or Shakti) requires three tasks of our prince: He must fetch a ring, gather millet seeds and find the apple. Yet he implicitly requires only one thing of her—to become his lover. This differentiation of tasks is typical of the female instinct and is easily distinguished from male requirements in love. Archetypally, the man requests that the woman be his lover, support him in all his tasks and be there when he gets back from the hunt. The woman needs proof that the man loves her and requires him to focus and even master her interests. Her requests often require superhuman abilities in fairy tales. In other words, simply focusing on what she wants is not enough. Trying to fulfill these needs with ordinary consciousness does not work. The hero needs his personal power, the help of his unconscious and his animal friends to solve the problems presented to him by his feminine partner.

When she throws her ring into the water and he cannot find it, his fish friends come to his aid in the last moment. If we consider the ring a symbol of the princess' relationship to her Self, then throwing it into the water means that she throws herself or the Self away in collective situations. She loses awareness of her individuality while she is dealing with social situations. The fish or body impulses retrieve the lost individuality because the pulsatile activities of the heart, stomach and breath express the repressed truths of an overly adapted person.

The analyst often depends on his fish to steer him correctly when the patient does not focus on central problems or act as he or she really is. The body picks up or reacts to the lack of genuineness and becomes cramped or ill. This reaction is the basis of the shaman's consciously taking on the problems of his patient and solving them in himself. In the analyst's case, how-

[68]Physics, of course, deals with time—at least theoretically—and brings it into relationship with matter and space in the general theory of relativity.

ever, such a *participation mystique* is accidental, or at least unsought. In any case, our partner's problems become psychological and physiological problems. The fish must pull the ring out of the water for everyone.

When the princess pours out her millet seeds for the hero to pick up, he is confronted with feminine reality. Millet seeds were originally used in making bread.[69] When they are spread on the ground, organizing dissociated material in everyday reality is required. Financial planning, ordering, cleaning and providing a good home are the challenges presented to our hero. At first the princess' requirements are felt to be too great and are rejected because they seem either impossible or unreasonable. But the hero's love for the princess forces him to undertake the impossible. Just as he is about to fail in achieving her reality needs, his ant friends come to help him. The nervous twitchings of the ants contain constructive plans which organize reality without even trying. If one stops solving an outer problem when one is exhausted, then the ants become alive. Like dwarfs of the night, nervous fingers carry energy and do the work.[70] Their ideas and impulses are related to a greater center than the ego, the Self.[71] Anything can be done as long as it belongs to one's individuation, but if reality must be mastered for ego purposes only, the work becomes unbearable.

Solving the problems of the ring and millet seeds draws our hero into everyday life. We can now see the value of his animal friends. His body instincts or dreambody powers find their greatest value in solving time problems, love difficulties and reality complexes. In contrast, the shaman or yogi hears the voices of the anima and animus inside the meditative trance and only tolerates them en route to nirvana. He does not befriend them or necessarily use them in his everyday life.

Our hero, however, does not wait for these voices to exhaust themselves. He does not say that they are only ordinary interests in the social world. Instead he serves them by focusing on their desires. He accepts his Maya as one form of body

---

[69]W.B. Crow, *The Occult Properties of Herbs*, pp. 12, 13.
[70]Fingers are *daktyloi* in Greek, the little dwarves and craftsmen who help the Earth Mother, Gaia, at birth.
[71]The solar hero Indras in Indian mythology is an ant. Angelo de Gubernatis, *Zoological Mythology*, p. 47.

energy which challenges another form. He sees his temporal "doings" as a part of his spiritual journey.

After he has found the ring and collected the millet seeds, after he has satisfied reality requirements with the use of his newly won dreambody awareness, the princess requires of him one last task. He must fetch the apple from the tree of life.

Apples (and nuts) were once the basic food of early Europeans.[72] Food was governed by the wheat and barley goddess, the earth mother Demeter.[73] Later, wheat, apples and nuts became the symbol of her body, just as bread and wheat today represent the body of Christ.[74] Apples are thus connected with the nourishing spirit of the earth goddess. They are the dreambody itself which is nourishing to life. An Indian symbol of the dreambody, the great Brahman, describes himself as nourishment, saying "I am the navel of immortality . . . I am Food. I feed on food and am its feeder."[75]

Amplifications show why apples symbolize the experience of the dreambody. The apples from the tree of life in our tale are connected to knowledge in the Bible story of Adam and Eve. The tree of Life in that story gives immortality. Hence, apples contain immortality and knowledge, timelessness and insight, body experience and wisdom. Thus eating apples awakens dreams in the body and transforms chronological consciousness.

The immense difficulty in obtaining nourishing body experiences is portrayed in many tales as the treasure that is hard to obtain. One thinks immediately of the famous Greek parallel to our fairy tale—the story of Hercules' theft of the golden apples from the tree of Life in the Garden of the Hesperides. Some versions of the tale tell about the guardian of the tree, the terrible serpent Ladon, which the earth mother Gaia placed in front of the apple tree to guard it from intruders.[76] She had originally given the tree to the gods Zeus and Hera on the occasion of their wedding.

We see here how the tree symbolizes the conjunction of the gods, Zeus and Hera. The eastern parallel to this conjunction is the union of Shiva and Shakti, which the meditator experiences

---

[72]Crow, *Occult Properties of Herbs*, p. 15.
[73]Ibid., p. 13.
[74]Ibid., p. 46.
[75]Heinrich Zimmer, *Philosophies of India*, p. 345.
[76]Kerényi, *Gods of the Greeks*, pp. 52–55. Ladon is sometimes portrayed as a nice river serpent who gives up his apples in a friendly way.

as a dissolution of personal existence and a union with what the alchemists would have called the *unus mundus*. But the Greek tale speaks about a horrible monster, Ladon, who blocks this experience. Ladon is, like the Godfather, a horned river serpent, master of energy flow within the psyche.[77]

The serpent guarding the great treasure is not only found in European tales but in the Indian story of the Kundalini.[78] This feminine serpent is, like Ladon, the guardian of the gate in the Muladhara, the root chakra of the spine. The mystery she protects is the Brahman, the secret of life. To the "profane" she is simply wild and terrible. She is pictured carrying a spear and sword and can kill animals. To the yogi, however, she is the differential capacity which cuts down unconsciousness, primitive drives, passions and sex. She cuts down blind instinctuality and prepares the way for the appearance of the Self. The Kundalini watches over the door to the Brahman, but she is also the creator of the world, the world mother who went to sleep and coiled up in the Muladhara after sparking the earth to life. As the snake she is an earth goddess. She is also called the "sad widow" because she has forgotten her heavenly origins. The yogi's job is to awaken her, to bring her to Shiva and help her to remember her divinity. The Kundalini is awakened to herself when the yogi meditates, "I am" or "Hansa," the word in Sanskrit for Brahman, and also swan.

The Kundalini is the princess in another form. Like the Kundalini, the princess needs the apple of life, the memory of its former existence, but like Ladon, paradoxically blocks the hero from obtaining these treasures. The princess' worldly tasks are the threshold which our hero must get over before he can find the apple.

If we translate the Kundalini and the princess story into psycho-physical terms, we discover a mythical account of bodily evolution. In creating and adopting to culture, body energy had to separate itself divisively from timelessness. Our snake—that is, our primate nature—seems to differ from that of other animals in that our body energy is capable of creating linear, chronological time. The human being can and must plot the future in order to survive. But in so doing, we have not only created vast technical cultures but we have cosmically isolated

[77]Ibid.
[78]Bohm, *Chakras*, pp. 59, 63, 64–66.

ourselves from each other, from animals, plants and the inorganic substratum of our universe. The nature of our consciousness and its ability to "do" are intimately connected with
our myth of loneliness which results from having forgotten our
origins.

While she was plotting out the future in order to secure her
stay on this earth, the Kundalini forgot she was once a paradisal
being, living in a timeless world. Her ability to "do" not only
prepared the future, it made her lonely and sick, because planning and worrying, when carried to extremes, annihilate the
vegetative nervous system and destroy the very goal they wish
to achieve—survival.

The body is troubled by two equal and opposite drives, both
trying to achieve survival. One is "doing" the creation of social
life, and the other is "being" atman, Self, Brahman, or others.
The hero's job is to solve the problems of the first by relationship to the second. First he must live through the suffering of
the Muladhara, the problems of this world, using the powers of
his body. His anima—that is, the cultural energies of his
body—need the apple from the tree of Life, the vegetative body
experience of timelessness.

But the hero cannot get the apples by himself. While lying exhausted in the forest in his quest for the final treasure, the
ravens appear and fetch the apple for him. Of course, the
ravens are the only ones who could find the apple. The experience of the timeless nature of the dreambody cannot be
reached by the ego alone. The body must find the apples within
itself.

More explicitly stated, once the abandoned Self in the body
has been touched by listening and caring for it, the body
awakens and acts like a partner of consciousness. Then the Self
in the body, the dreambody, becomes personal power, unfolds
its wings, stretches beyond its imprisonment in doings, and acts
out its dreams, its myths. One sees this happen in dreambody
work, as individuals follow their bodies, let them flow freely
and discover the myth behind personal life, the experience of
freedom.

Fairy tales, and myths amplifying these tales, tell us about the
evolution and patterns of the psyche. The study of these tales

has led researchers like Carl Jung and Marie-Louise von Franz to discover that the governing factor behind the myriad happenings in dreams and fairy tales is the tendency of the Self to become conscious. Different tales are like individual dreams, describing specific stages of the process of individuation, the Self's process of becoming conscious.

Physiological amplification of these same tales reveals patterns of dreambody behavior, structures in body life. Dreams and fairy tales are pictorial "theories," so to speak, behind body phenomena. In these tales we find different aspects of body problems. In the Mercury tale (Chapter 3) we saw how the dreambody spirit, in the form of Mercurius, struggles to free itself from cultural imprisonment, creating strange symptoms and requiring body work and imagination. In the Godfather tales we saw the adverse effects of treating the body as if it were a machine needing repair instead of a spirit requiring awareness. In "The Snake Leaves," a differentiation of body energies appeared in the form of two snakes whose harmony and functioning depend on consciousness. And in "The White Snake" tale we saw how individuation requires dreambody awareness which becomes a personal power and solves problems of everyday life.

All the figures of the psychic pantheon—the gods, snakes, animals, the anima, animus and Self—have physiological counterparts. From the viewpoint of body awareness, the images of dreams and fairy tales are symbols of psychological as well as physiological processes. The physiological corollary of the Self, the organizing power behind psycho-physical processes, is the dreambody. This power, restlessly yearning for development, appears in illnesses, body symptoms, compulsions and "doings."

The body, too, has an individuation process. Awareness of a dreambody occurs in specific stages, frequently beginning with illness and symbolized by the battle with the serpent, the love for the anima and animus. Each of these phases includes typical problems such as the possession by healing, the battle with doing, the expression of physical energy in unconventional ways in public life and the relativization of time itself.

Chapter 5
DREAMBODY THEORY

The foregoing chapters have described the dreambody as an empirical body phenomenon appearing in the practice of psychotherapy, as a dreamlike event manifesting in symbols and as an ancient shamanistic medical concept.

Dreambody work increases our understanding of modern psychology, verifies certain principles and alters others. In this chapter I want to show how such work may extend present concepts of psychology to include physiological awareness and a wide range of localized body signals as well as moods, dreams and visions.

I would like to assure the reader, however, that this chapter represents only a starting point, only one way of organizing facts and connections between the dreambody, dreams, body signals, archetypes and complexes. Present research is in the midst of such transformation and discovery that new principles are being defined more clearly daily and are connected more completely to older psychological theories. Under these circumstances any attempt to offer anything like a solid, completely satisfactory theory of psychosomatic phenomena would be premature.[1]

THE DREAMBODY AND CONSCIOUSNESS

The most basic concept in psychology—and probably the most difficult to define—is *consciousness*. When I refer to consciousness I think of a special awareness of proprioceptive body signals,

---

[1]Further developments based on the work of this chapter may be found in *Dreambody Communication* (Lemniscaat, Rotterdam, 1982), soon to appear in English, and *River's Way,* to be published. Also see my "Somatic Consciousness," in *Quadrant* (New York), Spring 1981.

fantasies and dream material. The greater the consciousness, the more ability there is to sense these signals and to integrate them into whatever is happening at the moment. For example, if someone has a sore throat which begins to ache during a conversation, integration of this signal might mean that the person should talk less, or should express himself in ways that do not burden the throat or voice.

The unconscious, by contrast with consciousness, cannot be discussed as a phenomenon of the moment because it is only discovered through retrospective reflection. In the moment the throat problem became conscious, it was no longer part of the unconscious. But we know that the unconscious exists as the unknown creator of dreams and body signals that are not yet integrated. Although it is difficult to give it an exact dreambody equivalent, the unconscious refers to involuntary body signals such as the heartbeat, involuntary signals that may be voluntarily controlled such as the breath and tics, as well as dreams, fantasies and visions. Voluntary action is conscious only when "doing" is under control. Otherwise voluntary action is governed by dream figures such as the animus, anima or shadow. Such action tends to be compulsive and split off from involuntary body life such as the heartbeat. The unconscious may also be thought of in terms of its personal or collective contents.[2]

The term *unconscious,* however, has been frequently used in the literature to refer to mysterious unknown or unknowable phenomena, which as a matter of fact can be easily observed by everyone. For example, the *unconscious* may manifest as secondary signals, that is, body phenomena lying just at the border of awareness. Primary signals are closest to consciousness and frequently include the content and meaning of what people are saying or trying to say. The unconscious then manifests itself in terms of secondary signals such as hand motions, head nods, unaccountable movements of the eyes and cheeks, blushing, and disturbances in hearing, as well as body

[2]The *personal* unconscious is related to civilized or learnable behavior and symbolized in dreams by people and by domesticable animals such as dogs and cats. The personal unconscious appears in dreams and muscle spasms that have assumed specific postural conditions in accordance with personal history, education, traumas and culture. The *collective* unconscious refers to essentially vegetative experiences which cannot be trained or manipulated and which remain relatively independent from consciousness. The collective unconscious may thus be symbolized by plants and undomesticable animals.

symptoms. Those secondary signals which we bring into awareness no longer represent the unconscious. I reserve the term
unconscious to mean that aspect of the dreambody which organizes dreams and body signals, as well as those signals that remain outside the perimeter of our awareness.

The *psyche*, on the other hand, is the total personality, the
combination of consciousness and the unconscious. It is identical to the dreambody when the unconscious is understood in
connection with its physiological equivalents. In other words,
the dreambody is composed of all the different degrees of
awareness. It has both physiological and dream aspects which
are easily differentiated from one another, and it possesses an
inner dichotomy which I have variously described in the
foregoing chapters as temporal and non-temporal experience,
chronological and non-chronological time, doing and being,
particle and field energies. This dichotomy creates tension but
also the potential for consciousness. Yet consciousness and the
unconscious only roughly correspond to particle and field
awareness, since consciousness itself is a result of the dreambody's dichotomy.

The center of consciousness awareness is the *ego*. The potential for this ego is derived from dreambody tension. The ego is a
useful term, especially for discussing the early stages of consciousness, because it may combat or combine itself with non-
temporal experience. In its primal state the ego senses non-
chronological experience, such as dreams and body signals, as
fate coming from the outside, as a force field impinging upon
mental and physical life. The ego is like a particle in the midst of
a foreign and bewitching field which exerts mysterious and irreconcilable pressures on existence.

At first the ego relates to chronological doing and seems to be
created from this "doing" which combats timelessness and
makes differentiations, boundaries, limitations, space and time
possible. From this ego's point of view—that of the present collective consciousness—the dreambody appears as a future experience, a weird exteriorized phenomenon hovering at the
limits of space and time. The ego in our culture is split off from
a dreambody. Further development makes it possible for the
Western ego to overcome its origins and associations to doing
and align itself simultaneously with both the particle and field
experiences of the dreambody.

We can say with the ancient Chinese shamans and physicians that "life itself is the beginning of illness,"[3] that consciousness develops from pain, discomfort, joy and extreme sensations. The ego awakens when the body is disturbed, since the disturbance means consciousness of a foreign element. Only later is it possible for the ego to introject and assimilate the foreignness, the body problems or psychic complex causing pain, and become like the disturbance in some way.

In early childhood one lives in paradise where disturbances are forgotten or not consciously registered. Ejection from this paradisal unconsciousness is connected with separation from the tree of immortality, with the sensation of pain, fear of death and the ephemeral existence. While at first the ego is characterized and created by the tension between doing and being, later this tension increases to the point where the possible cessation of life forces the ego to consider death, timelessness and life after death.

A strong motivation for combining doing with being, for integrating the unconscious and for working on the body begins only when death threatens. For this reason the basis for complete awareness does not appear normally until the late twenties or early thirties, although many individuals confront death at an earlier or later date.

In the beginning of dreambody consciousness, the body seems to become mysteriously ill, dreams disorder moods and everyday life, and the ego experiences itself as dominated by existence. Dreams occurring at this stage of development often portray how doing represses being.

Someone who did not know about dreambody work told me that his conscious problems involved a feeling that he was not giving himself enough love and that he was pressured by the collective to adapt. His body problems included a cramp in his back and a momentary need to stretch or swim. So he began swimming (on the floor). After a while he stopped because he still felt cramped. Then we amplified the cramp. He cramped himself so that his head was pressed in between his legs and his feet were twisted over his head. Because this position felt right, he stayed this way about ten minutes. Then he slowly came out

[3]Guido Majno, *The Healing Hand: Man and Wound in the Ancient World*, p. 244.

of this position and told me that he felt centered and meditative. He looked different, too. He was slower, more relaxed, and said that his back cramp had disappeared.

He began to talk about a dream in this relaxed, quiet atmosphere. He had dreamed that he was at a carnival and that suddenly he was called to a religious service. He associated to the carnival the collective pressure to behave in a certain way. To the religious service he associated a specific phrase he had once read about a living god inside oneself about whom one should not talk. He then interpreted the dream itself. The carnival was his own pressure to be someone he is not. The religious service was "calling" him to center. The interpretation was clear to him because he was now in the mood that the dream tried to create. Hence, instead of analyzing the dream from the normal ego or carnival point of view he immediately saw the dream's meaning because he was now at the vantage point of the dreammaker, which gave him perspective and insight. His doing was adapting, being nice to people. Not-doing, or not-being, for this person occurred as the back cramp, which was a sort of "calling" to a religious service.

THE DREAMBODY AND THE UNCONSCIOUS

We see how dreambody work can amplify and intensify dream interpretation and how dream interpretation can enrich and clarify the meaning of physical problems.

In dreambody work, dreams appear as pictorializations of body processes that are happening *now*. One experiences how the body is pressured by the dream world and how dreams are intimately connected to body problems. Often body work directly solves body problems, just as telling a dream may ease mental tensions (and indirectly body tensions as well). In the case described above, the backache disappeared because its message was integrated. The dream work strengthened the ego's grasp of the body work and enabled the ego to mentate upon the future. In dream work the past, present and future can be worked on; body work stresses the living present.

Body work cuts through a lot of junk in consciousness and gets right down to brass tacks quickly. The advantage to this is that the Self appears and a real relationship between persons often improves rapidly. Loneliness—the special loneliness of the Self, not the ego—is relieved because two Selves can communicate. Sometimes there is body contact between persons; often there is none. Physical contact is repressed by our culture because we divide the personality into mind and body, good and evil: The body has been made into the devil. Body communication remains undeveloped as a result of cultural repression. Either we illicitly fornicate or weakly communicate through a handshake, a kiss on the cheek or a final word sound.

The variations and differentiation of physical contact remain only a tempting potential in a semi-forbidden area. When this area is entered consciously, immediate relief occurs in many persons, especially those who are gifted in body communication. Just as there are thinking and feeling types, so there are also persons who communicate more completely through body contact than with ideas. Because body communication is an outlawed function, it often appears in especially talented "physical" persons in dreams in which the body is imprisoned or in an insane asylum.

Body work without dreamwork has advantages but also disadvantages. Because it drops right through ordinary consciousness, if body work is used without analysis persons do not learn to differentiate their everyday contacts or to see their power plots, games and masks. For the body, things happen slowly in body work. But for the mind, body work is rapid and Zen-like. One cannot follow it intellectually. Reviewing events therefore enriches insight and makes dream work the essential additive to body experience.

The less conscious the individual, the more the unconscious or the dreambody is experienced only as a force coming from the outside inducing disturbances into life. In the above case, the man felt that at the carnival a certain "field" (i.e., the dreambody) was calling, which seemed to exert a force on our dreamer, creating back pains. Briefly stated, the dreambody was sensed as a foreign force field by the ego. The field produced a cramp, a tendency to act in a certain way which is blocked by consciousness. These tendencies, inner forces and cramps are what Jung called *archetypes*. The archetype constellated at the carnival was God, the drive toward centering.

The structure of the field, the archetype, appears as the tendency toward specific movements, drives to fulfill certain physiological functions, dream images, fantasies and moods. Dream names for these archetypes may be the dramatic actions of the Self, anima, animus, King, Queen, Number, Birth, Death. The physical motions corresponding to these archetypes might be described in energetic terms such as centering, doing, non-doing, stretching, expressing, cramping, dancing, or quieting. A psycho-physical vocabulary for the archetypes does not yet exist.

The archetype is a field structure, a pattern that manifests itself in terms of dream images and body states. More simply stated, *the archetype is a compelling tendency toward a specific experience.* If the archetype or field pattern is not made conscious, then it becomes an enemy of the individual clinging to the chronological path. For someone in contact with the unconscious, the archetypes are body impulses and their wisdom. Otherwise, the archetypes become the root images of complexes and diseases.

The ego discovers the dreambody by interacting with it, not realizing at first that the dreambody is one's potential way of being. The interactions take one or more of many possible forms, depending on the nature of consciousness, the condition of the body, age, etc.

To demonstrate graphically the relationship between the ego and the dreambody's field, I use two-dimensional space-time diagrams emphasizing the temporal behavior of the ego and generalizing its movements in space (Fig. 52). (The three spatial dimensions are condensed into one dimension in these diagrams.) In any particular sketch, the archetype that represents the state of the dreambody appears as a spot in space-time. This representation applies to the chronological ego which has not yet become aware that the body and dreams are parts of itself. Spots in timespace are dream experiences and body sensations which occur in a given moment and place.

Let us pretend that the ego is represented by a line in time-space (called a world line by physicists). The dreambody's state, archetype or field structure is then a special irregularity or intensity within this field. The overall field may be conceived of in many ways. One may think of the fields in physics, the lines of force in a magnetic field around a magnet, the *li* or Chinese Tao patterns, or Chinese "dragon lines" which encompass everything in a given environment.

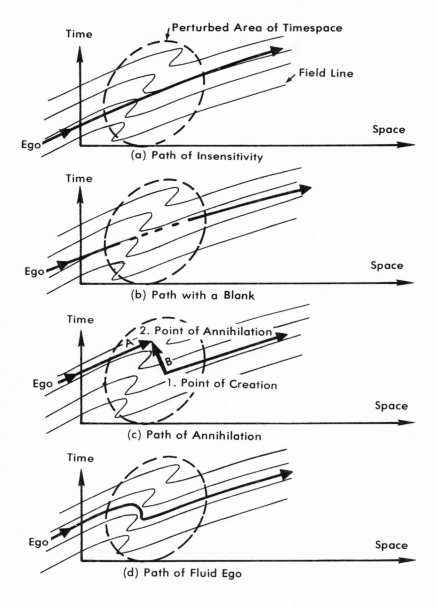

52. *Ego Traveling through Timespace*

In Fig. 52(a) we notice that the ego travels through a charged situation as if the situation did not exist. The ego notices neither body responses, fantasies or other disturbances which others in this field might experience and which the ego's body registers (as we could verify by attaching a measuring instrument which picks up body responses). Such a person tends to be insensitive, thick-skinned and can "walk over dead bodies."

In diagram (b) another type of interaction is shown in which the ego's path is strongly disturbed by interacting with the field. There is a blank in the middle of the field. The person cannot remember or explain what happened during a specific time. Such a situation might occur for example during an accident or a sudden illness. One suddenly comes out of the charged situation transformed, weakened or in shock. The strong disturbance of the ego's path is called *a complex,* a perturbation of chronological consciousness. The nature of the complex is given by dreams and body reactions which occur before or after the spaced-out period. Drug trips, near death experiences and comas are represented in (b). When a total anesthesia is administered during an operation, the nature of the resulting experience is told by the first reactions, feeling, visions and sensations occurring immediately after surgery. One woman, for example, upon awakening after a cancer operation, dreamed that she was being initiated into shamanism. Such a development was far removed from her consciousness at the time.

Another type of complex interaction between the field and the ego is portrayed in (c). Take the case of a man who complained about a nauseous feeling and a choking sensation in his throat. Dreambody work begins by amplifying the strongest and most immediate sensations—in this case, the choking feeling. The man amplified the choking feeling by gagging and began to regurgitate. But then the fantasy occurred that someone was choking him. The "dreamer" amplified this fantasy by grabbing and choking a pillow. After a minute the "choker" said to the ego, "I am furious with you because you are a weakling and will not follow me! I want you to do exactly as I say." The ego said, however, that it would not follow the message, it wanted to remain the way it was. Dreambody work in this case consisted of making conscious the split between the worlds.

In this situation the field or archetype is personified by the "killer," that is, the real personality, the individuation process. The ego is not ready to integrate the path of the Tao and decides to remain on its predetermined chronological course. Result? The next day the person "collapses" (to use his term) with a sore throat, fever and cough. What happened? Further work showed that the unconscious or the body signal increased itself, annihilating the ego, pushing it from its normal course and forcing it to follow another path. Another person might have integrated the path of the body, avoided illness and annihilation and thus voluntarily have changed his behavior.

Now let us look at the choking case schematically. In Fig. 52(c) the ego's stubborn path is represented by the forward motion in time of Line A: Line B is the killer, or generally speaking, the mood, vision, dream or body experience constellated by the field. Even before the ego has become conscious of the existence of the field, B has been created in the body at point 1 and moves along a collision path toward the ego. One feels pensive or ill and intuits that something is not right. By the time the charged field is experienced consciously in the form of body symptoms, B meets the ego at point 2 and annihilates it there. A dissociating interruption of attention, of focus and life result. One becomes ill, has a dream or even an out-of-body experience. So B is felt to be the enemy, intruder, illness or strange inexplicable turn of fate. The perturbation of the ego's course is a complex.

Complex is the name for a particular interaction in which the ego does not or cannot flow with the Tao, the dreambody. We see that a complex is formed by a combination of elements, such as a strong field and an inflexible ego.

Because the ego's focus and consciousness are disturbed by event B, after the annihilation we can no longer delineate the chronological sequence of events. Exact observations, objectivity and causal reasoning become irrelevant, because a chronological observer no longer exists. We must therefore content ourselves with understanding the total gestalt or archetype governing the situation. We are no longer able to know whether dreams precede body events or body problems create dream situations. Uncertainty rules the observation of every complex constellation. A scientific explanation of events that occur in diseased states is ruled out on principle. No one can say whether a magical situation produced an illness or whether bacteria created a numinous environment.

Body-mind, psyche-matter and time-space ideas are no longer determining factors and must be replaced by approximations, relatively inaccurate descriptions and overall archetypes when dealing with illness, fantasy and parapsychology. We have to accept the observer's personal description in terms of para-psychological, synchronistic, dream and body effects as psychologically determining but materialistically inaccurate.[4] I have noticed that people generally tell the truth but lie when dealing with a complex.

Whereas Figs. 52(b) and (c) show perturbations of a chrono-logical path (and are therefore complex reactions to the field), diagram (d) charts an ego which meets the field but steps out of its predetermined resolutions. This ego follows the direction of the field. A fluid line represents the path of the ego now. In-stead of being overwhelmed by a fantasy, suffering an illness or talking about a powerful experience, the present ego assimilates these experiences and unpredictably changes its behavior.

The chronological ego in Fig. 52(c) experiences the archetype or dreambody state as a complex perturbing its path. Because of its tendency to cling to linear time, this ego participates in creating illness, body symptoms, localized body motions, fan-tasies and even parapsychological effects. This ego pushes the psyche aside. The fluid ego of (d) also feels the strain and impression of a new field intensity but experiences this inten-sity as an invitation to change direction. Body reactions and fantasies are integrated into the moment and become the dreambody, the personality that becomes indistinguishable from the field around it. This ego does not fall ill, it "becomes" the illness, pain or dream, and in so doing transforms disease in-to life.

The transformation of the ego which incorporates the flow of the field is most difficult to describe. I remember a case in which a woman complained of chronic headaches, chest pains

---

[4]We can see from the foregoing that hard science or physics is limited to those experimental situations in which a strong archetypal constellation is not pres-ent. In other words, science and its laws do not necessarily apply to life!

and an inability to eat. These symptoms occurred regularly with great intensity whenever she had a vacation. During dreambody work her chest pain turned into a strangler in her fantasy who insisted that she get to work and labor day and night at a particular form of education which she had been avoiding. Immediately she realized what was called for and promised this voice that she would follow its message to the best of her ability. Her relaxed *persona* suddenly changed into a tensed body which looked ready for action. Her chest pain and choking feeling disappeared as she prepared to leave my office and get to work. This woman transformed herself. She was at a point in her life where a rigid form of relaxation could be given up in favor of hard work!

It is quite possible that the fluid person who lives with the body also becomes ill from the viewpoint of the chronological observer who experiences the dreambody as symptoms or disturbances of consciousness. However, the difference between the chronological viewpoint and the fluid ego is that the fluid personality does not experience body signals only as illnesses but also as potentially integrable aspects of life. This person "becomes" the disease and may reduce its symptoms or even witness their disappearance.

In cases where diseases remain, dreams often portray them as life itself. In terms of fairy tales, we might say that Death is asking to be an ally in life. There are many individuals who accept their chronic ailments as part of their own natures and let these body states create episodes existing at the edges of space and time. Many of these episodes are singular phenomena which can barely be imagined except under severe conditions.

In fairy tales and myths as well as in practical work, the final goals of the stories, rituals or processes seem to be the simultaneous experience of two states of consciousness which we may identify as doing and being, or time and timelessness. The prince finds the princess and eats the magical apple, two snakes intertwine forming the Caduceus, physical movement coincides with insight.

Because mind and matter, psyche and soma, timelessness and time leave the realm of speculation and seem to land on the solid ground of empirical reality in dreambody work, one is tempted to develop cosmic theories in which matter and psyche come together once and for all. Indeed, the development of the theoretical psychology which embraces all types of human phenomena is a goal for the future.

However, my experiences in dreambody work have taught me that theories, regardless of their usefulness, have at best intellectual value and at worst inhibit individuals from self-discovery and self-knowledge. Like the doctor in the Godfather tale, we too want to know the essential facts about the life principle. But we are forced to withdraw our questions because this principle forbids theoretical prediction. The essence of the dreambody can only be approximated through symbols, just as the essence of matter is only vaguely described in terms of theoretical physics. Uncertainty guards a secret from intellectual formulation and forces each individual to experience the world personally, as if nothing were known. Matter and psyche seem to be in constant union in dreambody phenomena, and appear separated only when we consciously consider dreams, symptoms or surprising synchronicities. The nature of this essence may be lawless. Its basic characteristic is, after all, Mercurial and changing. Nothing that can be said about it will hold true for long or for anyone but the speaker.

Chapter 6
WORKING WITH THE DREAMBODY

Some people follow and amplify body signals easily; others cannot. Children, for example, are ready right away because amplification seems to be a familiar game to them. When I asked my six-year-old daughter Lara to amplify her chronic case of hiccups, she soon made the hiccups worse and then imagined herself as a hiccup-maker. The hiccup-maker told her to come along and clean up her room, to be more useful instead of sitting in front of the television all day. Off she went, following the creator of hiccups. She started her cleanup chores, leaving the hiccups behind.

Like children, the people who have had some experience in psychotherapy are often prepared to experiment with their somatic life. But for the majority of suffering individuals it is not easy to drop their normal consciousness and focus on body signals.

When I ask a European or American adult who has been complaining about a physical ailment such as an ulcer or pain in the chest to experience the body, a wide range of embarrassing reactions may occur. Sometimes people giggle. Occasionally they say they do not understand. Often they ask that the question be repeated. Frequently they respond by changing the subject. At first there seems to be no logical reason for them to avoid the body problem. They appear willing to focus on the pain; after all, they argue and talk about the body problem. Why are they suddenly embarrassed when asked to take it seriously and find out more about it?

First of all, we must realize that many serious body problems often appear after years of living more or less "without a body." The average Western adult normally waits until illness strikes before he gets interested in physiology. And then when the body does express itself through disease, consciousness normally meets the invading uncertainty or terror with a league of arguments and rational explanations. The ill person may assure himself, for example, that the symptoms are not severe enough to worry about and then try to forget them. If they reappear or persist, he comes up with new theories to keep the problems at bay. He blames work, tension, fate; unconsciousness, insensitivity, and heredity. Bacteria or a lack of Vitamin C is his problem.

The suffering person may create his own solution at this point: he may repress the problem again or visit his physician. If the body problem is solved, then the story is usually finished for the sufferer, at least temporarily. But sometimes the problem continues, becomes chronic, or even threatens to be fatal. In this case, the suffering individual will try every possible medical solution. Then if these fail, he may be tempted to experiment with fantasy techniques or faith healers and go beyond the borders of his known rational world.

An individual's relationship to the body is a complex product of personal characteristics, cultural concepts, and prevailing medical theories. The body psychology is also connected to prevailing medical assumptions. These assumptions appear in the dreams one frequently has at the beginning of illness. Working on these dreams therefore becomes the first task of body work.

The prevailing collective medical assumptions are often symbolized in these dreams by doctors. When the physician in a dream has a positive connotation for the dreamer, the dream figure symbolizes among other things that the medical attitude associated to the doctor is important for the dreamer. In the simplest case, the positive inner dream figure symbolizes knowledge of the physical nature of the body which is not part of consciousness. For example, someone with a stomach ulcer who drinks three cups of black coffee for breakfast should realize that the mechanics and chemistry of the body are constructed in such a way as to produce violent reactions when coffee runs over an open wound in the stomach lining.

The inner physician may also have negative connotations. Often he is said to neglect the feelings of the patient, to have no relationship to the psyche and to be a mechanical personality. Such dream figures personify the dreamer's mechanical attitude toward the body which explains its nature in terms of rational causes and needs to change. Whether the inner doctor is "good" or "bad" at this stage of development, working on the body problems implies changing conscious attitudes. Much energy is often invested in projections onto a real doctor. He receives the brunt of the dreamer's personal problems and may be accused of being a notorious "quack" who deceitfully robs the patient by hiding information, or he may be transformed into a god capable of working miracles. One way or another the real doctor often finds himself in the midst of a web of embarrassing projections from which he is unable to extricate himself. The patient barely realizes that the negative or positive doctor partially represents unnecessarily mechanical or else unknown healing powers within himself.

As the physician archetype is made conscious through dream work, "thinking" about the body is gradually replaced by experiencing it. Dreams and body experiences now frequently present new attitudes and new methods of approaching the disturbing symptoms. I refer to these methods as spontaneously created manifestations of the dreambody.

Some dreambody processes tend to extrovert themselves and invite participation from a therapist, for example, spontaneous motions of the fingers and feet, spontaneous dance, visionary surgery, vision quest, and acupuncture.

WORKING WITH FINGERS

One of the most active and obvious modes of body expression consists of the uncontrolled movements of the face, fingers, feet and head. Spontaneous gestures of the fingers, hands and feet are overt expressions which are normally close to ordinary consciousness. We are indebted to Fritz Perls for discovering the language of the hands and feet.[1]

[1]Frederick Perls, *Gestalt Therapy Verbatim*.

Because motions of the hands and feet are readily accessible, it may be necessary in practice to differentiate between the body's consciousness and the ordinary intellect. For example, if one finger is vigorously scratching another and says that it is a nice day, then we can be certain that the intellect and not the finger has spoken. To clarify the difference between the mind and the finger, it is useful to identify with and actually imagine being the finger itself. If during this imagination the finger says that it wants to rip or attack someone, then we can be more certain that the body has spoken because its words are closely connected with the physical process that is happening.

I remember listening to a finger that began to speak in the middle of a boring conversation I was having. The finger was scratching the top of the chair where the person was sitting. After it was encouraged to continue the process, it finally said, "Dig! Dig deeper and deeper!" The finger's owner asked herself where she could dig deeper and then remembered that she had certain feelings which she had buried and which she did not want to dig up. The finger directed us to these important feelings, which naturally changed our conversation because its personality was now totally involved.

The night before this conversation occurred the woman had dreamed that a friend of hers had decided to build a house in the earth and for some reason had no interest in surfacing. After working with the fingers she herself was able to interpret the dream. Her body or her personality was split. One side of her wanted to remain on the surface of things (i.e., remain superficial) while the other was interested in digging deeper. Her finger motions and dream figures were both aspects of her dreambody's pattern of revealing feeling.

One way to test the validity of a dream interpretation is to check the emotional and intellectual responses of the dreamer during dream work and the subsequent course of the following dreams. An "ah-ha" reaction to dream interpretation or a definite change in the nature of subsequent dreams indicates that the original dream was integrated. The accuracy of body work may also be gauged. If body work has touched the dreambody, overt physical behavior immediately transforms. We have all noticed, for example, how many nervous motions such as tapping fingers disappear as soon as new ideas and actions are discovered. Finger motions, aches, pains and even lumps and wounds may change in body work. Consciousness also changes as the body evolves. It seems as if the body tends to compensate the prevailing conscious attitude of a given moment just as dreams compensate for general attitudes. In the previous case, for example, the woman's fingers stopped scratching as she consciously decided to dig deeper into herself.

In one case, dreambody work may consist of only nonverbal activity. In another case, a detailed account of the history and conscious situation of the patient is taken which ideally includes a description of chronic body problems and current physical difficulties. In this context, focusing not only on medical diagnosis but on the personal experience of physical symptoms is important. Through discussion, the individual situation and the dynamics between the individual, body signals, or dreams emerge. A particular case that comes to mind illustrates how dreams and body processes can couple in a simple way and how they both appear in dreambody work.

INNER PAIN

A man in his middle fifties suffered from chronically elevated blood pressure (diagnosed by his doctor as hypertension) and a nagging inner ear and throat infection. He told me that his blood pressure remained at 220/160 and that medication was of little help. Antibiotics alleviated the ear and throat infection temporarily, but as soon as he stopped them, the problem returned. The patient said he was not at all interested in psychology and was consulting me only because his doctor thought it might be worthwhile. He assured me that he was perfectly normal psychologically; his everyday life was entirely satisfactory except for an occasional feeling of being rushed in his work.

When I asked him what sort of sensations he was experiencing at that moment, he replied that his ear was bothering him. Taking this signal as a starting point for our work, I asked him to give me a detailed description of his earache. He said that it simply hurt. I asked him to tell me how it hurt, or what, in his imagination could make it hurt. In fact, what could possibly make the ear ache a little worse?

He commented that my idea of making the ear ache *more* was very strange, that he had been trying to do just the opposite. He had gone to his doctor to get medication to reduce the earache. He wanted to know just what I was driving at.

Since this man had an academic background and relied heavily on rational thought, I tried to answer his questions intellectually. I told him that my studies in Jungian psychology had taught me that amplifying dream signals with associations from everyday life often unravelled the meaning of dreams. Analogously, I had found that amplifying physical body signals physiologically often decreased the symptoms and explained them to the patient. I told him that amplification meant many things, but that in its simplest form, it meant increasing the strength of physical signals.

Because my explanation sounded reasonable to the patient, he agreed to try to amplify his earache. He felt blocked, however, and concluded that this approach was not for him. I agreed that body work is not suited to everyone and pointed out that there were alternative means for getting to the roots of body problems. I suggested that we spend some time getting to know each other better and that we talk a little about his feeling of being rushed.

Now I know that experiencing the body is not an absolute method to be applied at will under every set of circumstances. Its application, in contrast to more reflective techniques, depends on the personality of the patient and his relationship to his body, as well as on the background and personality of the therapist. There are times when body work absolutely cannot be done, and there are individuals who prefer to approach the body from the viewpoint of dream processes. In fact, body work may arise spontaneously in the midst of dream interpretation.

In any case, my patient then surprised me by stating that all paths were the same to him, and he wanted to make one more attempt to amplify the pain in his ear. After concentrating a few minutes, he said that it felt as if something were pushing his ear from the inside. I asked him to describe how this something pushed from the inside. He looked at me quizzically for a moment, closed his eyes, and began to meditate on the pushing. He took a deep breath and held it for what seemed a remarkably long time.

"That's it!" he exclaimed. "The pressure and pain in my ear can be recreated by holding my breath, closing my mouth, and trying to expel air through lips that won't open."

At this point I also began to experiment with holding my breath so that I would experience the sensations he described.

Consciously imitating an experience makes dreams and body problems more familiar to the therapist. Besides, if the therapist does not do so consciously, he will often do so unconsciously. Then he may intuitively guess the meaning of a dream without knowing exactly where his speculations came from, or he may feel ill without being able to relate his own physical symptoms to the condition of the patient. In contrast to these unconscious phenomena, the conscious empathy and amplification of such processes can be mentally relaxing and physically relieving to the therapist.

Thus the two of us experimented together for some time, alternately holding and expelling our breaths. After a while he said that his ear was "telling" the pressure to stop because (he giggled) it did not like being pressured or forced to do anything. The ear said, "Either you stop pushing or else I will ache!"

The man held his breath again, pushed, and then stopped. He sat meditatively in silence. Suddenly he opened his eyes wide with the excitement of discovery. He told me that the pressured feeling that gave him an earache was the same feeling he always experienced in his neck and ears when his blood pressure was very high. He concluded that his blood pressure problem must be related to the pressuring and pushing, the running around that he inflicted on himself. The ear and the rest of his body were crying out "STOP!" to the pressure. He said he now had an idea about how to use these ear and neck sensations to restrain his drivenness. He would try to change his life.

Before he left my office I asked him if he remembered any of his recent dreams. He reported that the night before he had dreamt about some policemen who were catching some mafia leaders. Immediately associating the word "mafia" to "pressure," he laughed and said that his ear must be like the police who were trying to catch the mafia-like pressure he kept putting on himself.

The reader may want to construct his own theory from this example. I too have formulated theories from individual cases over the past ten or fifteen years—theories that were often exploded when I heard conflicting experiences and facts from fresh cases. But the one idea that has survived this entire period is the concept of the dreambody.

In the case just discussed the dreambody manifested as pain in the ear and pressure in the neck, and as a dream of the police catching the mafia. The man's outer life, his earache, and his dreams seem to be different aspects of the same dreambody reality. Since psychic and somatic processes combine in the dreambody, the psychology of dreambody processes requires the integration of different types of analysis and therapy. Dreamwork by itself may not always produce changes in body processes, just as body work may not be uniformly satisfying from an intellectual or pictorial viewpoint.

Frequently training is necessary in order to learn how to communicate with somatic processes in their own language. In addition, it is not a simple matter for the therapist to relativize conscious prejudices about the body. Perhaps one of the most common and average assumptions is that the body's symptoms are indications of pathological phenomena that must be cured.

Amplification of body signals rarely supports this a priori sickness-healing hypothesis. Rather, it seems as if the body expresses information through these so-called symptoms, which apparently cannot be easily translated into anything but somatic language. Working with body signals over long periods of time with many different types of people tends to change the therapist's attitude toward the body. Ordinary sympathy for the suffering person or plans for healing the affliction are not always enough. Often the body demands nothing less than total life changes and altered states of consciousness.

In many cases a final or prospective attitude toward the body—in contrast to a causal, reductive healing philosophy—brings relief. Of course, the opposite may also be true. For example, a down-to-earth alteration of eating habits and a change in medication can create instant nirvana— especially for someone who psychologizes or spiritualizes the mechanics of the body. However, it would seem that the prospective attitude toward diseases and illnesses, which evaluates them as potentially meaningful experiences, is the missing element and farthest removed from conscious awareness. In such cases, a prospective outlook may contribute to unraveling the mystery of a disease, sometimes even reducing its strength. In the case of the man with hypertension and an earache, his blood pressure dropped during the following week from 220/160 mm Hg to 160/100, and the earache disappeared completely.

AMPLIFICATION

However, I do not want to stress the physiological changes accompanying dreambody work for several reasons. For one, I do not want to present amplification as a cure-all, even though healing is often a by-product of dreambody work. Healing is a specific goal, and amplification is chiefly a means for allowing the body to express itself. Also, I have no way of knowing whether or not physiological improvement is brought about by dreambody work and could not have been attained, for example, by simply meditating on the symptoms.

I can only state confidently that amplification establishes the fact that each person is at least two people: an ego with a mind and a body with another mind. And normally we are not of one mind! Dreambody work demonstrates that symptoms have meaning; they are not simply chaotic, destructive pathological states. Dreambody work is one method of communicating with patients whose consciousness is focused on body problems or whose consciousness is reduced or undermined by body problems. Finally, this work can be a powerful method of communicating with seriously ill people and with individuals especially gifted in body language.

But I do not mean to imply that amplification can only be applied to seriously ill people or to ones gifted in body talk. Amplification is a somatic approach to consciousness, just as dream work is a psychological approach to the individuation process. The ancient rituals and modern therapies reviewed in Chapter 2 demonstrated the broad spectrum of states in which somatic techniques can be used.

WORKING ON SKIN

I recently saw a businessman who complained about red blotches of eczema on his back. His everyday life and ordinary consciousness seemed to be in order, except for the fact that he always became nervous whenever he had to give a speech. Since he was primarily interested in his chronic body problem, we worked first with his body. At first nothing happened. Then, after a few minutes, he more or less unconsciously loosened his belt and breathed deeply. After sitting in a relaxed position for some time, his hands began to pull at his shirt. I pointed out to him what his hands were doing and suggested that he amplify his pulling and tug more consciously at his shirt. It was unnecessary for me to say more. Immediately he pulled at his shirt, took it off and lay down on the floor. Soon he began to roll around on the floor, vigorously rubbing his back on the rug. After a few minutes, he slowly stood up, turned around and showed me his back. "Look, Look!" he exclaimed. "My back is inflamed, all red, and look, it is on fire! It is excited and wants to be seen." When I repeated that it wanted to be seen, he said that his fire and excitement wanted to be seen and not kept "in the back."

He quieted down and seemed to be studying what had happened. Then he told me that in a recent dream a very nervous and uptight woman asked him to get into her car. He refused and ran out into a windstorm. He offered the following interpretation. He said that he had always been interested in how he appeared to people and therefore was often uptight like the woman in his dream. He was afraid to express himself emotionally. Hence his excitement "sat on his back." When he gets up to speak at the next meeting, he must let out his emotions, or rather "get into the windstorm."

There are symbolic and physiological aspects to this man's dreambody. The dream process in which he says no to the uptight woman and enters the windstorm was experienced physically as loosening his belt, irritating the eczema and demonstrating the resulting inflammation. The dreambody is the psychophysical process which is trying to dream itself, so to speak, into being.

The dreambody has been variously termed. When it is observed in meditation it appears in terms of the subtle body, i.e., inner designs of the nervous system. When looked at through visions occurring near death or in out-of-body experiences, the dreambody appears as a gaseous substance, a ghost, astral body or spirit. If we study the dreambody in fairy tales, then, as we have seen in Chapters 3 and 4, symptoms appear in terms of terrifying figures such as Death, Mercury, Godfathers and snakes. If we examine the dreambody in dreams then it appears as the figures and the processes creating action. In medicine the dreambody manifests itself in terms of physical symptoms; in body work it appears as the dreamlike process which tries to express itself through uncontrolled body motions.

In the eczema problem discussed above, cortisone treatment, the use of special soaps and a nonallergenic diet could not help that man's back because his excitement, inflammation and wind-god needed expression. If the eczema had disappeared under medical treatment, the inflammation would possibly have appeared in some other form. His body wanted the freedom to express excitement.

DANCE

The fingers, earache and eczema manifest local expression of the dreambody, but frequently the entire body becomes involved with potential movement. Feelings such as exhaustion, explosiveness, wildness, imprisonment, fatigue, restlessness or nervousness appear to be tendencies to move or "dance." When these dances unfold, surprising things often happen.

A colleague troubled by backaches reported to me that one of his first "dances" began with the feeling of stiffness and the need to bend, stand and exercise in a regular manner. After moving about for about five minutes one of the bending motions suddenly turned into an imaginary lifting and throwing action. As he continued to amplify these motions, he experienced the greatest satisfaction in throwing away an imaginary weight. Suddenly he had a realization. He was acting like Atlas, taking on the entire world, and he had to learn to throw off his load. He had unconsciously taken on too many patients. Now he realized why he had dreams of trucks with flat tires. He was overloaded.

The dancing Atlas is a good example of how creative dance combines physical exercise with psychological insight. Physical motions which bring satisfaction are always connected to meaningful potential psychological developments. Cramps such as backaches are mirror reflections of complexes such as power drives which overload the entire personality.

VISIONARY SURGERY

Often people suffering from body symptoms will readily relate a particular fantasy about their problems. Such fantasies commonly involve heart disease, cancer and infection, but often bits and pieces of special objects are imagined in the body. When surgical fantasies occur, the dreamer can begin active imagination by opening up the body and looking in to see what is wrong. Such spontaneous fantasies remind me of shamanistic practices in which the shaman uses drugs and trancelike states to imagine what is wrong with the body, to enter it with wisdom and imagination and to withdraw the evil by sucking or pulling.[2] Likewise the dreamer using active imagination also becomes a sort of shaman.

After pictorializing the disturbance lying beneath the skin, one may take many avenues in active imagination. The dreamer may take the object imagined to cause the disease as a dream figure and associate to it or discover its meaning, or experience physically the localized body disturbance.

I remember once seeing a man who was about to be operated on for cancer of the lymph glands. The impending operation naturally terrified the man and constellated surgical fantasies. The dreamer decided to consciously enter one of these fantasies and opened himself up. He saw a cramped ball in the place of his "cancer." He then became this ball—picking up the imagination in an active way—rolled himself up and stayed in a cramped "ball" position for a long time. When he finally asked himself what he was doing, he answered that he was protecting himself from fate. Suddenly he recalled the following story. Several months prior to the appearance of his "cancer," he had been involved in an automobile accident in which another driver smashed into him and was killed.

This accident reminded him in turn of other brutal acts of fate which had created powerful trauma in his life. His cramped position was an unconscious protection against further trauma. As I was able to see him only once, I discussed the work that was now indicated and recommended that he continue his imagination and develop a relationship between impending acts of

[2]Mircea Eliade, *Shamanism: Archaic Techniques of Ecstasy.*

fate and the "ball," since his cramp was cutting him off from life.

I later learned that his lumps disappeared and that he was not operated on. I never had a chance to check out the exact diagnosis of his condition or the circumstances around its healing. Such information was less important to me, however, than the fact that a trauma had become located in the body of this individual. Becoming conscious of this trauma may or may not have coincided with the disappearance of symptoms. Interest in "healing," while supporting the dreamer's momentary conscious interests, appears irrelevant in such cases because symptoms appear as diseases only to consciousness. The unconscious views most body signals as a natural part of the dream process.

There are cases in which the body even accuses consciousness of "causing" illnesses by maintaining unrelated and rational healing attitudes which isolate the body from the rest of the personality. "Healing" can be a potentially destructive attitude because not listening to disturbances or passing them off as pathological signals may force them to amplify themselves in order to be appreciated.

An interesting peculiarity of chronic cramps and lumps appearing in the "ball" story is their relationship to previous traumas. Chronic intestinal cramps, for example, frequently reveal fears generated in reaction to punishment occurring in childhood. However, I prefer not to make general theories about the physical locations of traumas because body work resists such simplistic theories. It is rare that a consistent pain gives rise to the same fantasy over an extended period of time. For example, a given heart spasm will produce (or coincide with) a painful fantasy about childhood one day but reveal a totally different fantasy about flying the next. Working on the body from the viewpoint of its own processes creates a varying picture of events and makes it difficult to verify theories which state that body problem X is caused or linked to psychological behavior. It seems to me that studies that indicate that certain types of behavior are related to specific diseases come from intellectual systems of thought removed from body experience.

Experience shows that the dreambody does not always operate mechanistically. For example, it is possible for consciousness to transform and for the body to retain its diseases.

Or a chronic disease may disappear apparently spontaneously without leaving any reasons for its disappearance. Some physical diseases may not have anything at all to do with the personal unconscious. Sick individuals whose dreams and body signals imply revolutionary cultural changes seem to suffer from the momentary collective unconscious or even from the world situation. I have even seen dreams and body work in which severe symptoms were related to the unconsciousness dreamers had in previous lives! When such dreams and body work occur, the only comment that seems to click with the dreamer is one that includes the idea of a previous incarnation, not one that relates everything to events during this lifetime. Individuals with such dreams and body processes have special tasks to accomplish in this world, but must realize that even the possible accomplishment of these immense tasks may not free them from their suffering.

THE EXISTENTIAL UNCONSCIOUS

When a person does not dream for long periods of time, the body becomes a crucial clue in unraveling the mystery of the personality. Body work becomes the primary tool when symptoms invade the foreground of consciousness whether or not dreams are present. Following the given physiological or dream material which dominates the foreground requires the analyst to be flexible. I remember once seeing a woman suffering from a nervous ailment which made her head shake constantly. Instead of working on her dreams she agreed to first amplify the shaking of the head. As she shook she fantasied that someone was standing beside her producing the symptom and saying "You think you know the way and never listen to anyone. Hence I shake you up and hope to make you uncertain." This voice made a strong impression on the woman. She admitted to me that she had not been prepared to take anything we might do seriously. Her shaking stopped for the remainder of that hour we talked.

This is another example of how the body gets the person in touch with what is happening in the moment. Dream work without reference to the body can also accomplish this although the connection to physical symptoms is usually less direct.

VISION QUESTS

Many experiences during analytical work indicate that the therapist's office is physically as well as psychologically limiting. While we can take these experiences symbolically and realize that a given therapy may be incorrect for a given patient, we should also consider the possibility that a psychotherapy that is bound to one place at a given time may be a product of the cultural setting.

The vision quest of an American Indian is a religious procedure in which the initiate searches for the solution to important questions by wandering into the wilderness, following the body through fasting, meditating and physical exertion.[3] The initiate returns from his quest with a visionary experience in connection with the original problem. In *Seven Arrows* for example, a quest is described in which a young man goes into the wilderness to find out what he should do with his life.[4] He comes to a cliff and, looking down, sees a young woman on the beach below and masturbates with her image in mind. On returning to the shaman, the young man at first says that nothing unusual has happened to him. But the wise shaman realizes that the masturbation experience was the "vision" being quested for and understands that the "vision" indicates that the young man should devote his life to teaching others about love.

I remember the vision quest of a man who constantly dreamed about running.[5] After he began to train in the art of long-distance running, his dreams still insisted that there was much to learn from this and that if he ran far enough he would find a magical woman. We decided to run together once and to remain watchful and see what we could discover. After a while he experienced stiffness in his back because, he explained, it was not rotating at the base of the spine in conjunction with the stride of his legs or the swinging motion of his arms. He felt stiff

---

[3]The vision quest is called "hunting for power" or "a meeting with the ally" in Castaneda's don Juan stories.
[4]Hyemeyohsts Storm, *Seven Arrows,* pp. 117ff.
[5]A description of the constellation of unconscious contents through long-distance running is found in Thaddeus Kostrubala, *The Joy of Running.* The relationship between meditation and running is described in Fred Rohe, *The Zen of Running.*

and compelled to rigidly face forward while running. But when
he allowed his back to rotate he realized why he was stiff.
When he swung with his running rhythm he felt he moved like
a woman with breasts and something said, "This is wrong, you
must remain a man!" However, his body said that the new
swing was a more restful and relaxed way of running. This
man's body was saying that he needed more anima, more
swing, more softness and less strength. Developing the art of
long-distance running required developing femininity and
loosening up his inhibitions. His vision quest revealed a magical
woman. Women suffer analogous inhibitions insofar as culturally accepted masculine characteristics are forbidden in female
behavior.

ACUPRESSURE

A surprising aspect of body work is that the body often asks
the therapist to partake in processes and to apply pressure or
massage to specific regions. I remember the case of a woman
suffering from crippling pain in the upper right side of her back.
After meditating on this pain she said that there was a pain-
maker standing behind her who was hurting her by pressing
and puncturing her shoulder blades. She stood up and wanted
to show me what this felt like and grabbed me by the shoulders
to show me what was happening.

As soon as this woman pressed my back her pain-maker
spoke and said that he was angry. So then we changed roles and
I pressed her back in the way she had done mine. Her immediate reaction was, "Oh, that is really good!" The harder I
pressed, the more she liked it. I repeated the pain-maker's "I am
angry at you," and continued to press. Then we reversed the
roles again and her pain-maker finally said, "I am angry at you
because you are vain!" Then the whole story came out. She said
that the pain-maker was right, she was vain, she was trying to
hold herself in a particular posture in order to look young and
beautiful and was not letting herself simply be. To make the
story short, she promised to change and the pain-maker told
her he would leave her alone.

I suspect that the need for acupressure often arises from the
therapist's unconscious loving or aggressive feelings toward the
patient. Most aggressive physical tendencies between patient

and therapist are repressed in psychotherapy or else subli-
mated. But many dreamers need a *real* shaking and pressuring.
This need is portrayed in their dreams, in their body fantasies
and in the tensions which they constellate in the *therapist's*
body. If these tensions are not made conscious they may contribute to making the therapist's body ill also.

Opening up or resisting fate are matters of the moment.
Opening up must feel right, be meaningful or be recommended
by dreams. Loosening contractions or lengthening muscles in
order to feel greater relaxation is senseless if a given person
requires a more rigid defense! Many body cramps arise in conjunction with the need for greater negativity and com-
bativeness. Hence, removing these cramps would only repress
energy which may "want" to create protection and armor. If
this energy is not rediscovered, then it sometimes appears in
less tractable problems than ones that manifest in the skeletal
musculature.[6]

MEDITATION

Many body signals are not experienced in voluntarily
operated musculature but appear in involuntary musculature
found, for example, in the heart and arterial system. These
signals are felt internally; they are proprioceptive and require
introverted sensing. Heart palpitations, blood pressure abnormalities, breathing difficulties and stomach malfunctioning are
examples of such signals. Problems of the vegetative nervous
system and dreams about snakes, worms, reptiles, plants or
even flying can indicate the need for greater consciousness of
the autonomic or vegetative nervous system.[7] Meditation upon
spontaneous breathing contacts this nervous system and has
been used since earliest times by Eastern shamans and yogis to
experience the world of the dead, flying through the air, returning to the womb and becoming a plant.[8] Breathing meditation
reduces ordinary consciousness and allows spontaneous fantasies to appear. At first these fantasies typically deal with daily

[6]I have come across dreams of persons suffering from cancer in which relaxation procedures were viewed as the "causes" of the cancerous condition.
[7]Many more symptoms and dream images relate to the autonomic nervous
system. I discuss these in Chapters 3 and 4.
[8]See Mircea Eliade, *Yoga: Immortality and Freedom,* Chapters 1–4.

problems such as love situations, financial difficulties and planning schedules. These existential fantasies occur simultaneously with slight variations in breathing rhythm and shallowness in inhalation. Working through these fantasies in meditation usually requires only minimal insight and immediately deepens breathing characteristics. Repressing internal dialogues, as Eastern meditations often recommend, can be psychologically impoverishing. Such fantasies return anyhow as soon as ordinary life is resumed.

Yoga and Zen meditation deal with internal dialogue by passively tolerating it until it disappears. Related body spasms, palpitations and fibrillations may also temporarily disappear, but reappear again as soon as one leaves meditation. If these fantasies are worked through, they disappear as in ordinary meditation but produce insight as well. Then a sort of vacuum or "hole" (to use don Juan's term for the absence of internal dialogue) appears which is then filled with experiences of the autonomic nervous system, experiences of far-out spaces, the Self, the language of animals, and mandala visions.

Generally speaking, one may deal with any visual or proprioceptive impulse which comes into the foreground of awareness while meditating. Hence, imagination may study internal dialogue if this takes precedence, or physical impulses if they disturb concentration on breathing. For example, a young physician with strong heart palpitations was disturbed by her heartbeat during meditation. When she focused on her heart, suddenly the physical experience turned into a vision of an eccentric old woman who was wobbling around in the middle of a town square and who was being stoned by onlookers because she was so unusual. This physician did not consciously accept her eccentricity, but tried instead to adapt to social standards. Hence, her heart palpitated as if it were being stoned.

In this case, experience and insight were simultaneous. The use of imagination in conjunction with subtle physiological impulses, however, often requires a great deal of patience.[9] Sometimes meditation apprehends physical impulses which immediately become associated with visions, while at other times a par-

[9]Carl and Stephanie Simonton, in "Belief Systems and Management of the Emotional Aspects of Malignancy," describe meditative imaginations in which medication for cancer is viewed as a positive force in combat against evil cancer cells. Such guided imaginations are unrelated to the spirit of active im-

ticular spasm or cramp seems to take years to spontaneously personify itself.

An interesting aspect of the fantasies derived from subtle physiological impulses is that although the imaginations give us a picture of what is going on in the body, they do not ensure that the psychological problems coinciding with the body impulses can be solved. Some physiological symptoms disappear as soon as they are envisioned but seem to reappear later in new types of symptoms. The apparent existence of fantasy related to deep body locations indicates that processes are not "problems" but deep physio-mythical foundations of a given personality. They are "just-so" descriptions of an individual's nature and are not necessarily meant to be "worked" on. However, solutions and transformations do frequently occur through having made a body process conscious. Such moments are fantastic and always coincide with deep-seated relaxations, opening the gates to a temporary *samahdi,* that is, a peaceful center. In these situations, consciousness is truly cleared and one achieves a momentary insight into the purusha, into infinity and timeless existence.

Meditation, however, is anything but a cure-all and has dangers too. Many people use meditation as a method for relaxation and may complicate a problem that already exists: lack of extroverted involvement. For such people the indiscriminant use of meditation may unnecessarily increase loneliness and contribute to reducing lively contact with reality.

DREAM INTERPRETATION

The interpretation of dreams is the last aspect of dreambody work I will discuss here. Normally dream work is not included in body therapies—probably because of two main factors. The first is that the interpreter may be insufficiently informed about the state of the patient's body. Only when the body's specific condition and the dreamer's individual description of body processes are taken into account is it possible to understand the connection between dreams and body processes.

agination in which the "dreamer" himself allows his own fantasy system to reveal what is going on in the body. In my experience with cancer fantasies, the medicines sometimes appear as the evil ones and the cancer as the Self. The attitude that disease is a bad thing which must be eradicated is a conscious concept that needs to be tested in individual cases.

A second reason for deleting dream work in body therapy may be due to inadequate knowledge of the physiological significance of symbols. Theoretically, however, dreams occur with a minimal interference from consciousness, so we should expect them to give us accurate pictures of body conditions. The trouble with this theoretical expectation is that in practice we know too little about the physiology of symbols. Hence we tend to focus only on the mental or verbalizable contents in dream work. We tend to assume that dreams do not deal with the body unless there are dream images of arms, legs, livers, kidneys, cancers and bacteria, that is, consciously defined diseases and organs. I now want to present some dreams which include more or less direct references to the body.

A man whom I see very infrequently and hence whose conscious problems therefore remain somewhat foreign to me brought the following dream fragment. It was the end of the world and everyone who was left had to swim for his life. The one chance for survival was to slip through a pipe into the world below. The pipe was narrow, and moving through it involved risk and danger. Nevertheless, he managed to arrive in the underworld and began to swim in the waters there. He associated the word "water" to the fact that he did not like to swim because he had trouble breathing while doing the crawl. To the word "pipe" he associated a shaman's instrument used to catch spirits. The interpretation which grew from these personal associations and which connected with his conscious problems was that he now had to become what he had projected onto the spirit, an unpredictable fluid being. His "spirit catcher" is still too narrow because his relationship to the imaginal world needs development.

Archetypal amplifications to his dream tell us that the end of the world means that his consciousness has now run out of fuel, in part because he—like the people in the Noah's Ark story —has not followed the designs of the creator. A new way of being is pressed upon him. Since this way is water, the old way must have been too dry or rational. The water scene belongs physiologically to the Swadhistana chakra, the second or water center located around the bladder in Indian subtle body theory. Trouble in this chakra means that there are flow problems, blood flow disturbances, menstrual or hormonal difficulties, trouble in passing water, kidney ailments, bladder infections, etc.[10] The inner experience of the water center includes fluidity, depth, and abysmalness which is why the whale or alligator appears in this chakra.[11] The dreamer's spirit-catcher or pipe also appears in subtle body symbolism as the *nadi* or conduit which connects the different centers. If the pipe is too narrow, meditation that increases awareness of this area is indicated.[12]

These archetypal ideas clicked immediately with the dreamer, who reported that he had chosen not to discuss certain physical problems even though they were forcing him into the hospital. He had prostate difficulties and could not urinate. Other dreams gave him specific meditational methods for contacting his body, or the spirit in the body.

Another dream dealing with the water center occurred in a younger man. He dreamed of an unhappy girl friend who felt inhibited and who led him to dancers carrying a bowl of water. He associated the bowl to a ritual initiation and rebirth, and the dancers to freedom. The water in the bowl brought him rebirth and a sense of increased knowledge in his fantasy. The water referred therefore to wisdom but also to fluidity, which is why dancers were carrying the water. This dream compensated a reality in which his fluidity was cramped because of severe social pressures and obligations. Physiologically, he also had symptoms of difficulty in urinating. The dancers were therefore associated with freedom, fluidity and body expressiveness which would be renewing to him. The unhappy girl friend symbolized his semiconscious unhappiness with his conscious situation and body's discomfort.

Dreams frequently include body symbolism. For example, a woman who fantasied about widespread lightning and thunder and a man who dreamed of being initiated by fire related to a sun god, had similar psychological problems. Both were too cool and unrelated and therefore needed greater expressiveness and explosiveness. Since the sun, fire and lightning belong to the solar plexus, or Manipura chakra, we would not be surprised to learn that these persons suffered from chronic

[10]Indian subtle body theory is presented in Werner Bohm's *Chakras: Lebenskräfte und Bewusstseinszentren im Menschen.*
[11]John Mumford, *Psychosomatic Yoga*, pp. 43–46.
[12]Bohm, *Chakras*, p. 72.

stomach ailments. The stomach overworked and created excessive digestive "fire" to compensate for a cool consciousness.

Knowledge of body symbolism is not always necessary to understand dreams—especially when the dreamer is consciously aware of body problems. For example, after having meditated on a skin rash, a man dreamed that flowers were growing out of his skin. He associated the shape of the flowers to the Liberty Bell. The imagination behind the skin sensations appeared in meditation and revealed the meaning of the skin problem. This man was too nice and needed liberation from his own decency. Here again we see how dreambody (i.e., dreams and body) signals seem to compensate for the state of consciousness.

Another man with a chronic intestinal cramp dreamed that this cramp made him bend over just as he was trying to walk past a group of homosexual men. He appeared to them as a homosexual. In the dream the man realized that the cramp was forcing him to confront his own homosexuality, his own eccentricity. In conscious life this man wanted to be "normal." His dream mirrors physical experiences of the dreambody as a power which literally presses the body into meaningful forms, actions and insights.

Far from being a ghostlike phenomenon occurring only at the time of death, the dreambody is the somatic experience of the total personality happening in the here and now.

Dreambody work is frequently very dramatic. Imagination, reflecting the pain of severe symptoms, generally deals with powerful emotions. When internal symptoms become the contents of imagination, existential messages often surprise consciousness, saying "Change or I'll kill you!" The mercurial spirit of the body panics consciousness, threatening the end of the world in its apparent effort to bring about instant change. Such dramatic fantasies seem to demonstrate that the unconscious uses the body to create changes which consciousness is too sluggish to make. Often the existential language of shamanism is heard in the voice of pain. Messages such as "Stop the world," "Take this moment as if it is your very last," and "Death is your only ally" are common telegrams which require action and reaction. The melodramatic sound of such statements comes partially from the fact that the unconscious does not know how to communicate to consciousness and partially from the fact that the conscious mind listens to nothing but itself. The dreambody must speak in terms of absolutes in order to achieve even the smallest change because of the insensitive nature of consciousness.

The more this consciousness changes, the more body signals and dreams are brought into awareness and integrated. Thus dreambody work promotes the process of individuation, which is a progressive unification of the personality. Individuation means that the eyes, skin color, lips, hand motions, body posture, voice tone, words and fantasies all manifest one and the same piece of information, the real personality, a living myth.

Chapter 7
FOLLOWING THE
DREAMBODY'S PATH

A central idea arises from this book: The body is dreaming. We discover that body processes will mirror dreams when the body is encouraged to amplify and express its involuntary signals, such as pressures, pain, cramping, restlessness, excitement, exhaustion or nervousness. Since a reduction of symptoms—and even healing— often accompany consciously unleashed body processes, we may conclude that in illness the body suffers from incomplete dreaming. The same unconscious contents that appear in dreams burden and activate the body with unexperienced forms of physical behavior and undetected insights.

The body processes, reflecting dreams and fairy tales, presented in this work indicate that human physiology is portrayed in mythology. The study of dreambody processes gives mythology a root in the flesh. We stand at the brink of new approaches to the body, approaches that are based on ancient concepts. Future research into the subtle physiology of symbols will reveal many insights about the body which I have only been able to hint at in this work. The little knowledge I have gained about physiology through the study of myths makes me painfully aware of how little we know about body processes and how much still remains to be learned about the physiological dimensions of well-defined psychological processes such as the animus and individuation.

We are entering a new dimension of psychological practice as far as the body is concerned. Thanks mainly to Jung, we are now able to follow consciously the developments of dream series. But we are only in an infantile state of knowledge when it comes to following the evolution of the body. The intricate rituals of Taoist alchemy, kundalini yoga and shamanistic medicine provide us with necessary information patterns. The procedures and myths of ancient rituals seem to be projections of the body's process of individuation—a new phenomenon which requires empirical observation and comparative mythological study.

The interaction between dream interpretation and body work enriches both. On one hand, dream interpretation, which already possesses a solid framework and the ability to increase consciousness, is rejuvenated by body work. This work extends the experiential dimension of dreams and generally increases the possibility for knowing the unconscious. On the other hand, dream work gives body processes a personalized, visual structure which —as far as I know—they have never had before in therapeutic work.

In addition to manifesting the mystery, dreams and distress of personal life, body processes universally challenge the outer world to change. For example, dreambody work reveals that our scientific attitude toward physiology, which tends to heal and diminish rather than decode messages, is a collective force whose misanthropy toward the soul represses individuality. But medical science is only a symptom of normalizing tendencies which fear the unexpected and shun the unknown. Since these tendencies often irritate the body and even propagate certain types of illness, we should expect greater tolerance of dreambody processes in the future.

Yet experience tells me that collective change is unlikely. Evolution in consciousness has always seemed minimal to me, technical achievements notwithstanding. Yet individual dreambody work encourages me to believe—against my better judgment—that transformation of the collective is imminent and necessary if a painful conflict between the individual Self and the community is to be avoided. Greater tolerance toward unpredictable behavior must take the place of rigid social pressure. Perhaps the popularity of drug experiences and unprecedented commitment to the new growth therapies already indicate that at least limited collective interest in the total personality has awakened.

The dreambody is released in every deep experience. These experiences often dissolve the boundaries of time, expanding it to infinity, almost abolishing its existence. Or they condense fate, drawing lifetimes together into minutes. Just beneath the unconvincing smile of today's world and the restless pacing in confined spaces, we find a force, the dreambody, whose potential charge threatens to explode, destructively quaking personal life, or to bend the rigid bands of collective regulation.

Studying the body's spirit starkly reveals an ailing king, symbol of an arid and routine life. If we refuse to let him either change or die, and ignore the revolutionary signs in dreams and body life, then fairy tales predict that extinction follows. The dreambody says: Disease and death—or change and individuation. But since individual change partially depends on at least minimal flexibility in the environment, the solution to many intractable diseases plaguing the public at any given time will depend not only on individual consciousness. Communities must learn to integrate apparently bizarre and even insane behavior. The lonely individual suffering from the uncanny power of some strange ailment should realize that he is troubled in part by the unlived life of a collective which has dreamed his body process into being.

Today those people who are either curious about the body or plagued by illness face a problem as old as man himself: the choice between illness and individuation. Whether or not an archetype annihilates the ego or creates a new pattern in life depends on whether or not one is able to step out of a predetermined course and follow the path of the dreambody. This path is full of unexpected events and difficulties. For example, interest in healing represses the body and looms as the first disturbance. Then comes the secret desire for nirvanic experience which is a shortcut to death itself. From the viewpoint of individuation, nirvanic experience that fails to interact with life is no greater than an impossible illness that only twists temporal existence into a tortuous course.

For those who are forced to abandon any attempts to heal or reach nirvana, one meaningful choice still remains: realizing illness as the beginning of individuation and of dreambody awareness.

BIBLIOGRAPHY

Ackerknecht, Erwin H. *A Short History of Psychiatry*. New York: Hafner Press, 1971.

Alain. *Yoga for Perfect Health*. New York: Pyramid Books, 1968.

Alexander, Franz. *Psychosomatic Medicine*. New York: W. W. Norton & Co., 1950.

Altshul, Victor. "The Ego Integrative (and Disintegrative) Effects of Long-Distance Running," *Current Concepts of Psychiatry* (July–August 1978).

Avalon, Arthur. *The Serpent Power*. New York: Dover Publications, 1974.

Bach, Susan. "Spontaneous Painting of Severely Ill Patients," *Documenta Geigy, Acta Psychosomatica,* Band 8, Basel, 1969.

Barlow, Wilfred. *The Alexander Principle*. London: Victor Gollanz, 1973.

Biofeedback and Self-Control. Chicago: Aldine, 1976.

Black Elk. See Niehardt.

Blatty, William. *The Exorcist*. New York: Harper and Row, 1971.

Bohm, Werner. *Chakras, Lebenskräfte und Bewusstseinzentren im Menschen*. Weilheim Obb., Otto Wilhelm Barth, 1966.

Boyers, Robert and Ortill, Robert, eds. *R. D. Laing and Anti-Psychiatry*. New York: Perennial Library (Harper and Row), 1971.

Brown, Barbara B. *New Mind, New Body*. New York: Bantam Books, 1975.

Butler, W. E. *How to Read the Aura*. Wellingborough, Northamptonshire: The Aquarian Press, 1967.

Capra, Fritjof. *The Tao of Psysics*. Bungay, Suffolk: Fontana, 1978.

Castaneda, Carlos. *Journey to Ixtlan, The Lessons of Don Juan*. New York: Simon and Schuster, 1972.

_____. *The Second Ring of Power*. New York: Simon and Schuster, 1977.

_____. *A Separate Reality: Further Conversations with Don Juan*. Simon and Schuster, 1971.

_____. *Tales of Power*. New York: Simon and Schuster, 1974.

_____. *The Teachings of Don Juan: A Yaqui Way of Knowledge*. New York: Simon and Schuster, 1968.

Cerney, J. V. *Acupuncture Without Needles*. New Jersey: Parker Publishing Co., Inc., 1974.

Charles, Garfield. "Ego Functioning, Fear of Death, and Altered States of Consciousness." In: *Rediscovery of the Body*. New York: Dell, 1977.

_____. ed. *Rediscovery of the Body*. New York: Dell, 1977.

Concise Encyclopedia of Living Faiths, R. C. Zachner, ed. Boston: Beacon Press, 1959.

Cook, Roger. *The Tree of Life, Symbol of the Center*. London: Thames & Hudson, 1974.

Crow, W. B. *The Occult Properties of Herbs*. Wellinborough, Northamptonshire: The Aquarian Press, 1976.

De Rola, Stanislaus Klossowski. *The Secret Art of Alchemy*. London: Thames & Hudson, 1973.

Dicara, Leo, ed. *Limbic and Automatic Nervous Systems Research*. New York: Plenum Press, 1974.

Dwarakanath, C. *Introduction to Kayachikitsa*. Bombay: Popular Book Depot, 1959.

Eliade, Mircea. *Shamanism: Archaic Techniques of Ecstasy*. London: Routledge & Kegan Paul, 1970.

_____. *Yoga: Immortality and Freedom*. Princeton: Princeton University Press, 1977.

Fabrega, H. and Manning, P. K. "An Integrated Theory of Disease: Ladino-Mestizo Views of Disease in the Chiapas Highlands." In: Garfield Charles, ed. *Rediscovery of the Body*. New York: Dell, 1977.

Feldenkrais, Moshe. *Body and Mature Behavior*. New York: International Universities Press, 1973.

Feldman, Peter. "Psychologische Deutung eines Odin Christus-Kreuzes aus Alemannischer Zeit." Thesis. Zurich: C. G. Jung Institute, 1978.

Franz, Marie-Louise von. See von Franz.

Goldstein, Joseph. *The Experience of Insight: A Natural Unfolding*. Santa Cruz Calif.: Unity Press, 1976.

Grimm, Jacob and Wilhelm. *Fairy Tales*. London: Routledge & Kegan Paul, 1959.

Gubernatis, Angelo De. *Zoological Mythology, or the Legends of Animals.* London: Trubner & Co., 1872; reissued, Detroit: Singing Tree Press, Book Tower, 1968.

Hannah, Barbara. *Encounters with the Soul: Active Imagination.* Santa Monica, Calif.: Sigo Press, 1981.

Harner, Michael J., ed. *Hallucinogens and Shamanism.* New York: Oxford University Press, 1973.

Homann, Rolf. *Die wichtigsten Körpergottheiten im Huan-t'ing Ching.* Goeppingen: Alfred Kümmerle, 1971.

Houston, F.M. *The Healing Benefits of Acupressure.* New Canaan, Conn.: Keat Publishing, 1974.

Howey, Oldfield M. *The Encircled Serpent, A Study of Serpent Symbolism in All Countries and Ages.* New York: A. Richmond Co., 1955.

Hyman, Selma. "Death-in-Life, Life-in-Death," *Spring 1977* (Zurich), 1977.

Jung, C.G. *The Collected Works of C.G. Jung.* Edited by Sir Herbert Read, Michael Fordham and Gerhard Adler. Translated by R.F.C. Hull (except Vol. II). Princeton (Bollingen Series XX) and London, 1953– . Cited throughout as *CW.* Volumes cited in this publication:

Vol. 2. *Experimental Researches.* Translated by Leopold Stein in collaboration with Diana Riviere. 1973.

Vol. 3. *The Psychogenesis of Mental Disease.* 1960.

Vol. 8. *The Structure and Dynamics of the Psyche.* 1960.

Vol. 9. Part 2. *Aion: Researches into the Phenomenology of the Self.* 2nd edition, 1968.

Vol. 11. *Psychology and Religion: West and East.* 1958.

Vol. 12. *Psychology and Alchemy.* 2nd edition, 1968.

Vol. 13. *Alchemical Studies.* 1967.

Vol. 14. *Mysterium Coniunctionis: An Inquiry into the Separation and Synthesis of Psychic Opposites in Alchemy.* 2nd edition, 1970.

Vol. 16. *The Practice of Psychotherapy.* 1954.

Vol. 18. *The Symbolic Life: Miscellaneous Writings.* 1975.

_____. Individual writings, with relevant volume of the *Collected Works* (see above):
"Commentary on 'The Secret of the Golden Flower,'" *CW*, Vol. 13, pars. 1–84.

"Further Investigations on the Galvanic Phenomenon and Respiration in Normal and Insane Individuals" (with Charles Ricksher), *CW* 2, pars. 1180–1311.

Letters of C.G. Jung. Edited by Gerhard Adler in collaboration with Aniela Jaffé. Princeton (Bollingen Series XCV), Vol. 1, 1973; Vol. 2, 1975.

Man and His Symbols (with M.-L. von Franz, Joseph L. Henderson, Jolande Jacobi, Aniela Jaffé). New York: Doubleday, 1964.

"The Philosophical Tree," *CW* 13, pars. 304–482.

"Psychological Commentary on Kundalini Yoga," *Spring 1975*. (Zurich), 1975.

"Psychology of Eastern Meditation," *CW* 11, pars. 908–949.

"A Review of the Complex Theory," *CW* 8, pars. 194–219.

"The Spirit of Mercurius," *CW* 13, pars. 239–303.

"Synchronicity: An Acausal Connecting Principle," *CW* 8, pars. 816–968.

"Psychology of the Transference," *CW* 16, pars. 353–539.

Keleman, Stanley. *Your Body Speaks Its Mind*. New York: Pocket Books, 1976.

Kenton, Warren. *Astrology, the Celestial Mirror*. London: Thames & Hudson, 1974.

Kerényi, Carl. *The Gods of the Greeks*. London: Thames & Hudson, 1961.

———. *The Heroes of the Greeks*. New York: Grove Press Inc., 1962.

Kostrubala, Thaddeus. *The Joy of Running*. Philadelphia: Lippincott, 1976.

Krishna, Gopi. *The Kundalini: The Evolutionary Energy in Man*. Berkeley: Shambala Publications, 1970.

[*New*] *Larousse Encyclopedia of Mythology*. London: Hamlyn, 1972.

Legeza, Laszlo. *Tao Magic, The Chinese Art of the Occult*. London: Thames & Hudson, 1975.

———. and Rawson, Philip. See Rawson, Philip.

Lipowski, Z.J. "Review of Consultation Psychiatry," *Psychosomatic Medicine* (New York) (March, April), 29:153–171 (1967).

Lockhart, Russell A. "Cancer in Myth and Dream," *Spring 1977* (Zurich), 1977.

Lowen, Alexander. *The Betrayal of the Body*. New York: Collier Books, 1973.

Lu K'uan Yü. *Taoist Yoga: Alchemy and Immortality*. London: Rider & Co., 1972.

Majno, Guido. *The Healing Hand: Man and Wound in the Ancient World*. Cambridge: Harvard University Press, 1975.

Manning, P.K. See Fabrega, H.

Maple, Eric. *The Ancient Art of Occult Healing*. Wellingborough, Northamptonshire: The Aquarian Press, 1977.

Die Märchen der Weltliteratur. F. van des Leyen, ed. Dusseldorf/Köln: Diederichs Verlag, 1960.

Meier, C.A. "A Jungian Approach to Psychosomatic Medicine," *Journal of Analytical Psychology* (London), VII, 2 (1962).

Michell, John. *The Earth Spirit, Its Ways, Shrines and Mysteries.* London: Thames & Hudson, 1975.

Mindell, Arnold. "Being Dreamed Up," *Sundance Journal* (to be published).

_____. "The Golem," *Quadrant* (New York), VIII, 2 (1975).

_____. "Synchronicity, An Investigation of the Unitary Background Patterning Synchronous Phenomena." *Dissertation Abstracts International,* 37, 2, 1976.

Miyuki, Mokusen. "*The Secret of the Golden Flower,* Studies and Translation." Unpublished thesis. Zurich: C.G. Jung Institute, 1967.

Monroe, Robert A. *Journeys Out of the Body.* Garden City: Doubleday / Anchor Books, 1971.

Moody, Raymond. *Life After Life.* New York: Bantam Books, 1976.

Moreno, J.L. *Who Should Survive?* New York: Beacon, 1952.

Muktananda, Swami Baba. *The Play of Consciousness.* California: Shree Gurudev Siddha Yoga Ashram, 1974.

Mumford, John. *Psychosomatic Yoga.* Wellingborough, Northamptonshire: The Aquarian Press, 1976.

Netter, Frank. *The CIBA Collection of Medical Illustrations,* Vol. 1, *The Nervous System.* Ciba, N.J.: 1968.

Niehardt, John G. *Black Elk Speaks: Being the Life Story of a Holy Man of the Oglala Sioux.* New York, 1932. (Paperback edition, Lincoln Nebr.: University of Nebraska Press, 1961.)

Onians, Richard. *The Origins of European Thought About the Body, the Mind, the Soul, the World, Time and Fate.* New York: Arno Press, 1973.

Ortill, Robert. See Boyers, R.

Ornstein, Robert, ed. *The Nature of Human Consciousness.* San Francisco: Freeman & Co., 1973.

Patanjali. *Yoga-sutras.* Poona: Anandasrama Sanskrit Series XLVII, 1919.

Perls, Frederick S. *Gestalt Therapy Verbatim.* Lafayette, California: Real People Press, 1969.

Picard, Barbara. *French Legends, Tales and Fairy Stories.* London: Oxford University Press, 1966.

Pierrakos, John. *The Energy Field in Man and Nature.* New York: Institute for the New Age of Man, 1971.

Prichard, Robert. "Structural Integration, (Rolfing)." In: Garfield Charles, ed. *Rediscovery of the Body.* New York: Dell, 1977.

Purce, Jill. *The Mystic Spiral: Journey of the Soul.* London: Thames & Hudson, 1975.

Rawson, Philip. *Tantra: The Indian Cult of Ecstasy.* London: Thames & Hudson, 1973.

_____ . and Legeza, Laszlo. *Tao: The Chinese Philosophy of Time and Change.* London: Thames & Hudson, 1973.

Rechung, Rinpoche. *Tibetan Medicine.* Berkeley: University of California Press, 1970.

Redfearn, J.W. "The Patient's Experience of His Mind," *Journal of Analytical Psychology* (London), XI, 2 (1966).

Reich, Wilhelm. *Character Analysis.* New York: Farrar, Strauss & Giroux, 1968.

Rendel, Peter. *Introduction to the Chakras.* Wellingborough, Northamptonshire: The Aquarian Press, 1974.

Ricksher, Charles. See Jung, C.G.

Rohe, Fred. *The Zen of Running.* Philadelphia: Lippincott, 1976.

Rola, Stanislaus Klossowski de. See De Rola, Stanislaus Klossowski.

Rolf, Ida. "Structural Integration," *Confinaia Psychiatrica,* XVI, 69–79 (1973).

Saezle, K. *Tier, Mensch und Symbol.* Munich: Bayrischer Landwirt Verlag, 1965.

Schouten, Jan. *The Rod and Serpent of Asklepios.* New York: Elsevier Publishing Co., 1967.

Schutz, Will and Turner, Evelyn. "Bodymind." In: Garfield Charles, ed. *Rediscovery of the Body.* New York: Dell, 1977.

Scott, R.D. "Notes on the Body Image and Schema," *Journal of Analytical Psychology* (London), I, 2 (1956).

Sharkey, John. *Celtic Mysteries, The Ancient Religion.* London: Thames & Hudson, 1975.

Simonton, Carl and Simonton, Stephanie. "Belief Systems and Management of the Emotional Aspects of Malignancy," *Journal of Transpersonal Psychology* (1) 29–47 (1975).

_____. *Getting Well Again.* Los Angeles: Tarcher Inc., 1978.

Simonton, Stephanie. See Simonton, Carl.

Spence, Lewis. *The History and Origins of Druidism.* Wellingborough, Northamptonshire: The Aquarian Press, 1971.

Storm, Hyemeyohsts. *Seven Arrows.* New York: Harper & Row, 1972.

Suzuki, Shunryu. *Zen Mind, Beginner's Mind.* New York: Weatherhill, Inc., 1976.

Tansley, David V. *Subtle Body, Essence and Shadow.* London: Thames & Hudson, 1977.

Thera, Nyanaponika. *The Heart of Buddhist Meditation.* New York: Weiser, 1962.

Tolkien, J.R.R. *The Lord of the Rings.* London: George Allen & Unwin, 1969.

Turner, Evelyn. See Schutz, Will.

van der Leyen, F., ed. *Die Märchen der Weltliteratur.* Dusseldorf/Köln: Diederichs Verlag, 1960.

Veith, Ilza (trans.). *The Yellow Emperor's Classic of Internal Medicine.* Berkeley: University of California Press, 1966.

Vogel, Virgel. *American Indian Medicine.* New York: Ballantine Books, 1970.

von Franz, Marie-Louise. *Introduction to the Psychology of Fairy Tales.* Zurich: Spring Publications, 1973.

_____. *Number and Time.* Evanston: Northwestern University Press, 1974.

_____. *Time.* London: Thames & Hudson, 1979.

_____. "The Process of Individuation." In: C. G. Jung. *Man and His Symbols.* New York: Dell, 1971.

Werblowsky, R.J. Zwi. "Judaism, or the Religion of Israel." In: R. C. Zachner, ed. *The Concise Encyclopedia of Living Faiths.* Boston: Beacon Press, 1959.

Wheeler, Charles E. *An Introduction to the Principles and Practice of Homeopathy.* Bradford: Health Science Press, 1971.

The Yellow Emperor's Classic of Internal Medicine. Translated by Ilza Veith. Berkeley: University of California Press, 1966.

Zachner, R. C. "Introduction" to *The Concise Encyclopedia of Living Faiths.* R. C. Zachner, ed. Boston: Beacon Press, 1959.

_____, ed. *The Concise Encyclopedia of Living Faiths.* Boston: Beacon Press, 1959.

Ziegler, A. "A Cardiac Infarction and a Dream as Synchronous Events," *Journal of Analytical Psychology* (London), VII, 2 (1962).

Zimmer, Heinrich. *Philosophies of India.* In: Joseph Campbell, ed. Princeton: Princeton University Press (Bollingen Series XXVI), 1969.

ILLUSTRATION CREDITS

Frontispiece © BBC Hulton Picture Library
1. Kangra, Himachal Pradesh, c. 1820. Gouache on paper, 12 x 9 in. Sven Gahlin, London.
2. Jeff Teasdale, Durham.
3. Sonia Halliday.
4. Nataraja. Tamilnadu, 10th century, Chola Dynasty, Bronze. Los Angeles County Museum of Art: Anonymous Gift
5. Spring Festival of Flowers, Baha; near Pakur, Santal Parganas, Bihar. Photograph: George E. Somers.
6. Arasu Bhuta. Attavara, Mangalore. Martha Bush Ashton.
7. The nadis, diagram, Tibet.
8. Self-portrait drawing by Albert Dürer, Germany, 16th century. Kunsthalle Bremen.
9. Kalighar painting, India, c. 1880. British Museum, London.
10. Astral man from Robert Fludd's *Collectio operum*, 17th century.
11. From MS. of Liber divinorum . . . by St. Hildegarde of Bingen, Germany, c. 1200. Biblioteca Statale, Lucca.
12. Zodiacal Man, page from MS. "Les Très Riches Heures" de Duc de Berry, early 15th century. Musée Conde de Chantilly. Photographie Giraudon.
13. Zodiacal man from Codex vaticanus B, Aztec, 15th century.
14. Swami Baba Mustakaneda *Play of Consciousness*, p. 100. Copyright 1978. Gurudev Siddha Peeth, Ganeshpuri, India.
15. © Copyright 1953, 1972 CIBA Pharmaceutical Company, Division of CIBA-GEIGY Corporation. Reprinted with permission from THE CIBA COLLECTION OF MEDICAL ILLUSTRATIONS by Frank H. Netter, M.D. All rights reserved.
16–22. Reproduced from *The Serpent Power*, Ganesh and Co., Madras 17, India.
23–25. Reproduced from *The Secrets of Cultivation of Essential Nature and Eternal Life* by Chao Pi Ch'en as reprinted in *Taoist Yoga, Alchemy and Immortality*, Lu K'uan Yu. Samuel Weiser, Inc., York Beach, Maine.
26. Copyright 1973 by the Wellcome Trust. Reprinted by permission of the University of California Press.
27. See 26.
28. Reprinted from *The Healing Benefits of Acupressure* by F. M. Houston. Copyright © 1974 by F. M. Houston, D.C. Published by Keats Publishing, Inc. New Canaan, CT. Used with permission.
29. See 23–25.
30. Hermetic transformation from Samuel Nor-

ton, Mercurius redivivus, 1630. Edinburgh University Library.
31. Rajasthan, 18th century. Inks on paper, 19 x 13 in. Ajit Mookerjee, New Delhi.
32. 1738, frontispiece of David Coster. A. Bicker Caarten collection, Leyden.
33. Detail of the Nine Dragon Scroll by Ch'en Jung, dated 1244, Sung dynasty, ink and slight color on paper, h. 18½". Museum of Fine Arts, Boston (Francis Gardner Curtis Fund).
34. Pharmacopoeia Lillensis, ed. II, 1694, frontispiece by Jacques Robilat after a design by Arnould de Vuez.
35. Shunga print, Meiji, Japan, School of Utamaro, early 19th century.
36. By the painter Pamphaios, from Gerhard "Auserlesene griechische Vasenbilder," II, 115.
37. a. Cave drawing from Val Camonica, Italy c. 4th–3rd century B.C. Ananti Camonica Valley, London 1964, pls. 24, 25. b. Stone relief of Cernunnos, flanked by Apollo and Mercury, from Reims, Marne, France, 2nd century A.D. Musee Saint-Remi de Reims.
38. Maerten de Vos, wash drawing, 1594, Municipal Print Room, Antwerp. Sted. Pretenkabinet. Photo t'Felt, Antwerp.
39. From de Rola's *The Secret Art of Alchemy* (Rosarium philosophorum, 16th century). Stadtbibliotek, Vadiana.
40. Anatomical drawing, India, 1st c. A.D.
41. See 15.
42. Yggdrasill, the Mundane Tree, frontispiece of "Northern Antiquities" by Bishop Percy, 1847.
43. Lama Govinda, *The Foundations of Tibetan Mysticism*, Rider, London, 1960.
44. Detail of bowl, Elamite, late Sassanian, A.D. 226–641.
45. Woodcut, Swiss, 1615.
46. Illustration in Vincenzo Cartari's "Le Imagini de i Dei de gli Antichi . . .", Venice, 1571.
47. Francesco de Giorgio, bronze, c. 1489. Staatliche Kunstsammlungen, Dresden.
48. Possibly Sarnath, India, c. 475 A.D. Los Angeles County Museum of Art: From the Nasli and Alice Heeramaneck Collection: Museum Associates Purchase
49. By Bernini, Italy, 17th century. Palazzo dei Conservatori, Rome.
50. From *Tantra, The Indian Cult of Ecstasy*, Phillip Rawson, Thames and Hudson, 1973.
51. Calcutta, 19th century. Watercolor on paper, 18 x 11 in. Victoria and Albert Museum, London.

INDEX*

*Italicized page numbers indicate illustrations.

209